TYING SMALL FLIES

Ed Engle

STACKPOLE
BOOKS

Published by
STACKPOLE BOOKS
5067 Ritter Road
Mechanicsburg, PA 17055
www.stackpolebooks.com

Printed in China

First edition

10 9 8 7 6 5 4 3 2 1

Library of Congress Cataloging-in-Publication Data
Engle, Ed, 1950–
   Tying small flies / Ed Engle.—1st ed.
       p. cm.
   ISBN 0-8117-0082-8
   1. Fly tying. 2. Flies, Artificial. I. Title.
SH451 .E54 2004
688.7'9124—dc21

2003011874

CONTENTS

FOREWORD

I've been friends with Ed Engle for something like thirty years now, during which we've done very little together besides fish and talk, not necessarily in that order. I know we met in some kind of writers' workshop in Boulder, Colorado, in the early 1970s, but my earliest clear mental picture of us together is of the Cheesman Canyon stretch of the South Platte River back in its golden age when large, cagey, wild trout were stacked in the pools like brood fish at a hatchery.

These were trout that could sometimes be enticed to eat a tiny little fly tied to a 6X or 7X tippet, but they were smart. The Canyon had been a popular fly-fishing spot for the better part of a hundred years, and it had a reputation for being tough even before it became Colorado's first ever catch-and-release area in the mid-1970s.

Ed got into small flies back then not because they were the coming fashion, but because most days they were the only way we could catch those fish. The South Platte had always been known as a small-fly river. (It's been a classic tailwater, complete with huge populations of very small bugs, since the construction of Cheesman Dam in 1905.) The old-timers used to say you could fish a whole season there and never use anything larger than a size 16. Later that was revised to size 18, then 20.

Then as now, talented fishermen and tiers were refining their small-fly skills on the Platte and passing their knowledge along to the trout through endless hours of fishing. It was what they'd now call a simultaneous learning curve, and somehow the fish always seemed to stay a step ahead of most of the guys with fly rods, including me. Ed will admit to his own slow days on the South Platte and other small-fly rivers—both back then and now—but he was always one of those rare few who did better than most. That's because he was, and is, a thoughtful tier and a keen observer. He also spent a lot of time on the water, and he just had the touch.

Ed has been into small flies in a big way for at least three decades now, pretty much since hooks smaller than size 20 became standard items in the fly shops. He's tied them himself by the thousands, fished them, guided other people fishing them, watched the development of hooks, materials, and techniques, and soaked up ideas like a sponge. As a journalist he has chronicled the work of dozens of other tiers and fishermen. By now, he knows more about small flies than anyone else I can think of.

When the fishing is difficult, there's the temptation to get complicated with fly patterns, but Ed's tastes run to the practical side—simple patterns tied simply and sparsely. As he puts it, "Tying small flies is fly tying stripped to its most basic elements." That comes from being a working guide who needs flies he can manufacture quickly and easily and lose without regret. Guide patterns are notoriously pared down to the basic triggers that make fish bite—size, flash, color, shape, whatever—without the added frills designed to catch fishermen or show off your skill with a bobbin and scissors.

Ed has learned through years of experience that you're much better off with flies that suggest the bugs in the subtlest, simplest way than with highly detailed copies on size 26 hooks: those things that make even the best tiers break out in a cold sweat at the vise. The patterns in this book are all flies that are known to work, and they're presented as is. Nothing has been fancied up for publication.

I've always liked the way Ed thinks about fishing and fly tying. He naturally wants to catch fish, but beyond that he's just curious. He has the ability to see things that are right there to see, but that most of us nonetheless manage to miss, and when his curiosity is piqued—which seems to happen almost daily—he's likely to "go to the books," as he says, to learn more.

A science background and his life as a writer have taught him which books to go to and where they're likely to be found. A lot of them are in his own library, including some dusty old fishing volumes that contain many of the observations and ideas we wrongly think of as "new."

Ed likes solutions and he'll go to great lengths to find them, but he also has a finely honed sense of humor, so he can still enjoy those mysteries that stubbornly remain mysterious. All that gives his writing the kind of depth and perspective you seldom see in fishing books.

You can use this book as a straightforward pattern bible—and you'll probably want to—but before you start flipping around to specific fly recipes, I suggest that you sit down and read it cover to cover first. What you'll find is an incredibly detailed, meticulously researched essay on all aspects of small-fly tying and fishing that, if you're like me, will light up the subject in ways you hadn't thought of before.

I especially like the way the flies are placed in context. How and why a fly was developed, by whom, on what river, and in response to what situation tell you much more about flies than just the recipes for tying them. Enough of that kind of detail strung together can begin to give you an overall rationale for which flies to tie, when they might be useful, and ultimately how to design your own patterns or intelligently fiddle with existing ones.

There's a lot here, all of it useful, and I know for a fact that the research took years, both on and off the water.

I've tied and fished with small flies for about as long as Ed has—although not with his intensity or, I'm sorry to say, his success rate—and before I read this book I'd have told you I understood them. But apparently not. There was a lot I didn't know and a lot more I hadn't thought of in quite that way before. This book did for me what the very best tying books can do: It made me want to run to the vise to tie, and then run to the river to fish.

John Gierach

INTRODUCTION

Several years ago a small-fly tying enthusiast came up to me at a fly-fishing show and asked when I was going to compile the "Small Flies" columns that I'd written for *Fly Tyer* magazine into a book.

"I'm tired of always having to go through all those old issues to find a pattern that you talked about," he said. I'd never really thought much about gathering the columns into a book, but when I looked back through them as a whole I realized that they formed a fairly comprehensive small-fly tying primer.

The first "Small Flies" column appeared in *Fly Tyer* in the Summer 1996 issue, and one has appeared quarterly in most issues since then. The inclusion of a "Small Flies" column at all was a leap of faith for Art Scheck, who was *Fly Tyer's* editor at the time. Although some fly fishers and fly tiers were aware of the potential of small flies through the writings of Vince Marinaro, Ed Koch, Arnold Gingrich, and Darrel Martin, it was clear in 1996 by just looking at the way that fly hook sales dropped off under size 16 that fly fishermen as a whole had not yet embraced the idea that a tiny fly could land a sizable trout.

I don't know what possessed Art to run the column, but I was happy he did. I'd cut my fly-fishing eye teeth on Colorado's premier small-fly river, the South Platte, and I had a head full of ideas about how small flies should be designed, dressed, and fished. And where I didn't have ideas or knowledge, I knew other small-fly aficionados who did. Over time the columns grew into laid-back little "talks" predominantly about the theory and practice of tying small flies, with occasional asides on how to fish them. I had a lot of fun writing the stories because they always made me

feel like I was up on the river talking to my buddies about what was working, what wasn't, and why.

That's how the book *Tying Small Flies* came about. I struggled with the title at first because I didn't really think the chapters in the book covered the gamut of small-fly tying from A to Z. As I mentioned earlier, I'd always seen it more as a compilation of little talks about various aspects of tying small flies, but the more I looked at the chapters and their contents the more I realized that they really did cover a lot of ground. I've organized the chapters roughly into small-fly history, tying tools, and certain important small-fly tying materials at the beginning of the book. The middle and bulk of the book addresses specific patterns and tying techniques for various aquatic insect groups and other tiny trout foods. Toward the end of the book you'll find chapters on general-purpose small-fly patterns, and finally a little ditty on tying size 32 flies. I think the book lends itself to skipping around from chapter to chapter and tying whatever catches your eye, but it also works if you start at page 1 and work your way to the end. Better yet, use the flies presented here as models of various small-fly styles and modify them for your own regional small-fly fishing needs.

If you read the original "Small Flies" columns in *Fly Tyer* magazine, you'll notice that I've edited, revised, and merged many of them here. In a lot of ways the original columns were an inventory of the state of small-fly tying as I knew it at the time. I've deleted inaccurate or grossly out-of-date information. I've retained anything that I think is historically interesting. You'll find the story of origin of the South Platte Brassie (now known generically as the Brassie) as told by a descendant of one of the inventors. Rim Chung tells you how he came up with the famous RS-2 and his unique way of attaching the tails to the fly and dubbing it.

Another thing you'll notice if you read the original columns is that I've retaken many of the original photographs and in a number of instances I've revised the step-by-step tying photographs. When I was retying some of the flies for the book, I was surprised to notice that I was tying them differently than I did when I wrote the columns. Like all fly tiers, I think my technique has improved a bit with the passing years and the new photos show the results of those improvements. In addition, new materials and better fly-tying threads have allowed me to do some things I couldn't do when some of the columns first appeared.

It's the year 2003 now and a lot has changed since I wrote my first "Small Flies" column in 1996. The definition of "small fly" has continued its march toward smaller and smaller hook sizes. New, less bulky materials seemingly become available every week. And most significantly, many more fly tiers are interested in tying and fishing small flies. There has literally been an explosion of interest in small flies over the past few years.

What hasn't changed over the last seven years are the reasons I tie and fish small flies. I started fishing small flies on the South Platte River thirty years ago because I had to. The trout required it. I dutifully responded. But a transformation took place over the ensuing years. I found myself fishing small flies not only because they caught trout, but because of their elemental simplicity. If you tie small flies you know that once you get used to the tying proportions and just being able to see the tiny small hooks, actually tying the fly is not difficult. You just can't tie that much stuff to a small hook. Techniques for tying the few materials that you can attach to the hook tend to be pretty basic. At first I tried to complicate my small-fly designs because they just seemed too simple, but I ultimately came to appreciate that very simplicity. It means that there is that much less between me and the trout. Tying small flies and fishing them is fly fishing stripped to its bare essentials. There's no room for fluff, no way to fake it, and there is nothing added. It's the trout and me with as little in between as possible. That's the way I like it.

A book like this doesn't just come out of a single fly fisherman's head. A lot of people have helped me along the way. Nothing would have been possible if Art Scheck and the past and current publishers of *Fly Tyer* magazine hadn't taken a chance on a small-flies column. Joe Healy and Dave Klausmeyer, also editors at *Fly Tyer,* helped edit and publish some of the original columns, too.

An exchange of ideas, techniques, and tying "tricks" is essential for any fly tier. This book's very foundation rests on what I've learned from A. K. Best, John Gierach, Stan Benton, Jim Auman, Jim Cannon, Matthew Grobert, Kent Brekke, Neil Luehring, Randall Smith, Dick Talleur, Brooks Handly, Dusty Sprague, John Betts, Bob Miller, Lynn Allison, Rick Murphy, Rim Chung, John Barr, Scott Fraser, Gary Willmart, Pat Dorsey, Roger Hill, Dale Darling, Shane Stalcup, Roy Palm, Al Beatty, John Flick, and Peter Kummerfeldt.

The most difficult task I had when editing this book was to put the word "late" in front of Gary LaFontaine's name—so I didn't do it. Those of you who knew him will understand why.

Bill Merg and Chris Helm made important contributions to the information presented here on tying threads. Bill Chandler supplied historical background on the development of the South Platte Brassie. Rick Hafele helped out on small mayfly entomology.

Bill Chase, Bruce Olson, Jeff Pierce, Scott Sanchez, and Brent Bauer provided important information about small hooks.

Dave Wolverton and Mark Lewis freely provided technical support that made the photographs in this book possible. Master carpenter Doug White crafted an ingenious platform for my cameras that greatly improved the quality of the close-up photography.

I'm sure I've inadvertently left some names out of these acknowledgments. If yours is one of them, please accept my thanks for your contributions.

Finally, nothing ever gets done without support on the home front. My sweetheart Jana Rush's good-natured response to the inherent crankiness that comes when someone (me) decides to try to take 450 photographs of size 20 and smaller flies was angelic. My mother, Bernice Engle, and my sister, Carolyn Reyes, also lent their wholehearted support to the project.

My thanks to all of you.

CHAPTER ONE

Small Flies History

"Small fly" is a relative term. In 1900 a fly tied on a size 16 or even a size 14 hook was considered small. As the technical ability to manufacture small hooks has improved with each succeeding generation of fly tiers, it seems as though small flies have gotten "smaller." And that's true, at least in terms of the availability of high-quality commercially produced small hooks.

I might note, however, that the smallest hooks manufactured a century ago were indeed small. Hooks we would describe today as size 18 were available in 1900. It's hard to make comparisons, though, because the scales used by turn-of-the-century hook makers differ from those used today. I have an illustrated 1902 Hardy Brothers Catalogue that advertises Hardy's "Midgets" dressed on special hooks in sizes 000, 00, and 0. The smallest "midget" (000) is the equivalent of a modern size 20 hook with a rather short shank. It would pass for a small fly even by today's standards.

It's interesting to note that fly fishers and tiers well before the twentieth century were quite aware that trout ate very small naturals and that they needed imitations that matched those tiny insects. Thoughtful anglers did not cast size 14 flies at trout rising to size 24 midges.

Several years ago my friend Paul Schullery, the fly-fishing historian, told me that I should be very careful about saying "tiny flies weren't possible or practical until recent times." Schullery mentioned British fly-fishing historian Jack Heddon's research on the early flies of England, which indicated that by 1800 anglers were using flies as small as modern 16s. In addition, Heddon said that the generally accepted notion that early nineteenth century flies were larger and dressed on heavier hooks than modern flies is a misconception. Actually, the hooks were made of finer wire and it was possible to make them quite small. Schullery comments that a single horsehair leader could have handled hooks down to size 20 or smaller.

Schullery says that before the industrial revolution a lot of people "made their own stuff," including hooks. If you wanted to *buy* a hook, you could obtain it from local craftsmen who produced "commercial" hooks. If a fly tier had wanted a hook smaller than those commonly available, he could probably have made it himself or had it made; the materials and technology were there. It's also possible that something really different like a size 20 or 24 hook might never have been noticed outside the local area where it was crafted, especially if it didn't make a hit on the commercial market. The point here is that fly tiers are a pretty innovative bunch. In Paul Schullery's words, "In the 700 or so years since fly fishing emerged as an identifiable kind of sport in Europe, think how many people must have seen fish rising to tiny flies and tried to figure out how to get in on that."

I'm just glad that small-fly crazies have been around for a while. I like the idea that back in 1890 some oddball small-fly nut like me may have shown his fly box to a fellow angler and heard him mutter the same words that I still hear today: "You're not serious, are you?" Let's face it—until very recently those of us who tie and fish small flies have been considered the eccentrics, crackpots, and weirdos of the sport.

In the early 1970s, when I first started fishing tiny flies on Colorado's South Platte River, it was still difficult to find high-quality hooks in sizes smaller than 22. We used 7X Maxima tippet material then that rated a hefty half-pound test. As late as 1980, British anglers were still unconvinced about the merits of the Americans' "fine art of midge fishing." Brian Clarke and John Goddard, in their classic *The Trout and the Fly,* admonish readers that in their view "the persistent use of tiny rods and gossamer leaders to large fish regardless of circumstances, is not simply an affectation, but an unsporting affectation. No fish should be cast to with tackle clearly unlikely to land it, in the circumstances in which the fish is found."

The popularization of small flies in the United States is most commonly credited to Vincent Marinaro, who included a chapter titled "Minutiae" in his classic 1950 work, *A Modern Dry Fly Code.* Marinaro was a devotee of southeast Pennsylvania's challenging limestone creeks, whose brown trout happened to be small-fly gourmets. Along with other Pennsylvania anglers such as Ed Koch, Charlie Fox, and Ed Shenk, Marinaro laid the groundwork for American

small-fly tying and fishing. Ed Koch's book, *Fishing the Midge,* published in 1972, was the first to deal exclusively with fishing small flies.

The first small-fly patterns to come out of Pennsylvania were often scaled down, modified versions of larger flies. Ed Shenk's well-known and still productive No-Name Midge isn't much more than a stripped down Adams—grizzly hackle fibers for the tail, muskrat body, and grizzly hackle. Ant patterns that had previously been tied in size 16 were scaled down to size 22 to imitate smaller ants. The practice of reducing successful larger patterns to small-fly scale is still an important part of small-fly imitation today.

Arnold Gingrich further piqued angler interest in small flies when he described the 20/20 club in his 1965 collection of essays, *The Well Tempered Angler.* Membership in the 20/20 club required that an angler catch a 20-inch trout on a size 20 fly.

Although the word was out, widespread interest in small flies didn't really occur until the 1980s. The increasing popularity of fly fishing had led more and more anglers to America's famous spring creeks and tailwaters, where small flies are crucial to success. Fly fishing's increased popularity was also coupled with a revolution in synthetic fly-tying materials.

Up until the 1980s, most fly patterns were tied primarily with natural materials. Small-fly patterns by their nature tended to be simple; you just couldn't tie that much "stuff" to a size 20 or smaller hook. This was particularly true when tiers tried to use bulky natural materials. The commonly available 6/0 threads seemed to fill the tiny hooks by themselves. Small-fly tying theory had to deviate from the increasingly popular attempts to tie visually exact imitations of the aquatic foods that trout eat. There just wasn't enough room on the hook for all the materials necessary to create exact imitations.

Small-fly tiers began to closely study the tiny naturals and how trout took them. They tried to determine what it was about a particular midge, small mayfly, microcaddis, or tiny terrestrial that triggered the trout to take. They stripped their patterns down to the basics and concentrated on impressionist patterns that emphasized the triggers. Synthetic materials turned out to be perfect. Synthetics were considerably less bulky than natural materials, which meant that small-fly patterns could be tied with slimmer, more natural silhouettes. Bright new synthetics such as Krystal Flash were just what tiers needed to reproduce the bright gas bubbles that many aquatic insects, especially the tiny midges of the order Diptera, use to inflate their pupal shucks to carry them to the water's surface for emergence. Nowadays, most of us can't imagine tying without items such as Z-Lon, Zing, Microfibetts, microchenilles, Antron, polypropylene, and ultra-fine synthetic dubbings. Couple these materials with threads available as small as 14/0, remarkable natural materials like genetic hackle and cul-de-canard, and high-quality small hooks in a variety of styles, and the possibilities are endless.

Angling with small flies has come a long way, too. The strength of tippet material has increased dramatically—6X commonly tests at three pounds or more. Hooks are stronger. All of this means that larger trout can be quickly played to net and released unharmed back to the river or lake using the smallest hooks.

It's even beginning to look like small flies may enter the mainstream of fly fishing. Hook manufacturers still say that their sales drop off significantly for sizes smaller than size 16, but the gap is narrowing. More fly tiers are exploring the part of the hook rack in their local fly shop that holds the 22s and 24s, and some are even seeking out the 30s and 32s. I'd venture to guess a few are even making small hooks in their basements. I sure hope so.

I welcome the company. I like eccentrics, crazies, crackpots, and weirdos—especially if they tie small flies.

CHAPTER TWO

Small-Fly Hooks and Tying Tools

There have been remarkable advances in the design and manufacture of small hooks over the past thirty years. Size 18 and smaller hooks are sharper, stronger, and more available than ever. Innovative small-hook design, coupled with the increased strength of 6X and 7X tippet material, is why tying and fishing small flies continue to gain in popularity.

This isn't to say that there weren't good small hooks thirty years ago. Mustad was making excellent dry-fly hooks down to size 28, and they were available anywhere there was any interest in small flies. Partridge of Redditch also made some high-quality small-fly hooks, though availability was limited. VMC hooks, manufactured in France, were also excellent, but even more difficult to find. Partridge and VMC products were so coveted by American small-fly enthusiasts that a kind of tiny-hook black market developed.

The big difference in small-fly hooks today is the availability of so many more design styles. In the 1970s you had to be content with standard-wire hooks down to a size 18 for nymphs or extra-fine-wire dry-fly hooks to size 28. There were few variations in shank lengths available. And that was it. Manufacturers are now offering straight-shank hooks in a variety of lengths and wire diameters, as well as curved-shank hooks.

I should say that while I have a healthy respect for the technical requirements necessary to design and manufacture high-quality hooks, I am not a techno-freak. I'm not one of those guys who perform bench tests to determine the strength, flexibility, or sharpness of a hook. I leave that to the trout. The truth is that I usually lose fish through the normal comedy of angling errors such as poor line management, badly timed strikes, or overexcitement, and not because small hooks bend or break. Most of these hooks become damaged when I snag something other than a fish and pull too hard in an attempt to free the fly.

This doesn't mean that I haven't been seduced into reading some of the literature of hooks. I know what round, Limerick, Sproat, and Sneck bends are and where most of those bends are likely to break. I've studied discourses on hooking leverage as regards angle of pull and effective shank length. I sometimes even find myself perusing hook-strength graphs. But literature and theory aside, the bottom line for me has always been what happens on the trout stream.

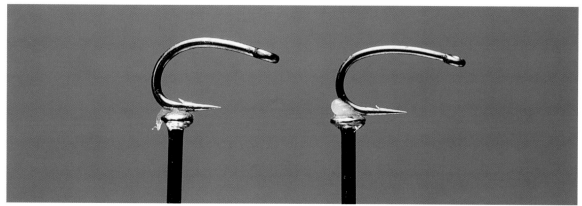

Hook manufacturers now offer small hooks made from heavier wire. The Tiemco TMC 2488H (left) introduced in 2001 uses 2X heavy wire. The original Tiemco TMC 2488 (right) uses fine wire.

Most of the ideas I have about small-hook use, strength, and design come from empirical experience on the water, rather than in the lab.

My main criterion for small hooks used to be finding wide enough gaps. Now, the greatly increased pound-test strengths of fine tippets has me looking for hooks with heavier wire, too. The very fine wires used for some small hooks may not be practical now. Thanks to today's high-quality genetic hackle and super floatants, you can tie dry flies on stronger, heavier-wire hooks.

I talked with Bill Chase of Angler Sport Group, the importers of Daiichi hooks, about the use of stouter wire. He said that he's noticed an increase in the number of small-fly tiers requesting small, stout-wire nymph hooks and that Daiichi is exploring the use of heavier wire for their smaller hooks.

"It's getting to the point where the tippet is stronger than the hook wire," Chase said. "We've been looking to beef up our wire in the smaller hooks. It appears as though the heavier wire doesn't affect flotation much and it adds about a quarter more dead-weight strength to the hook." Chase said it would be nice to remove the stigma of the hook being the "weak link" in fishing small flies.

Most of today's small hooks have round bends (sometimes called a Perfect bend), but there are

some that have sweet-looking Sproat and Limerick bends. The eyes on small hooks come turned-down, turned-up, and straight (sometimes called a ring eye). The differences in hooking ability and strength among hooks with different eye styles are marginal. Some anglers believe that hooks with turned-up eyes in effect have larger gaps than those with turned-down eyes, but I haven't found that this makes a difference when it comes to hooking fish. The most important considerations for hook-eye style are the fly design and personal preference. You don't want a turned-up eye on a micro-parachute pattern, for instance, because it would be more difficult to tie the fly to the tippet.

My choice of hook mainly depends on the insect I'm trying to imitate. If the natural is curved or swimming when the trout take it, I tie the imitation on a curved-shank hook. If the bug is a bit long, I select a long-shank hook. It's most desirable when the hook has the right shape *and* a wide gap, heavier wire, and/or an offset point.

After you determine the hook style you want, you need to find the right size. This isn't as easy as it sounds. I once spread a box of size 24 dry-fly hooks across my desk to compare size. Although the widths of the gaps were relatively constant, the lengths of the shanks varied widely—often as much as 2X or even 3X. As it turns out, this is

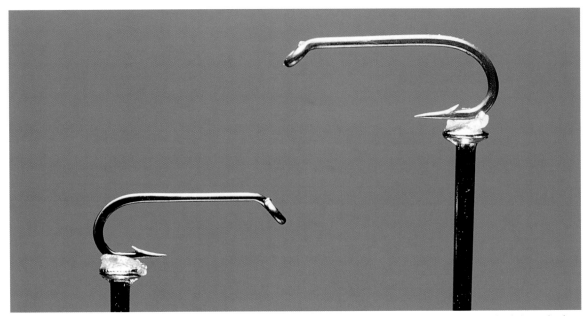

Actual hook sizes vary among manufacturers. The Mustad 94840 (left) and Tiemco TMC 100 (right) are both designated as size 20.

true for most of the major hook distributors because they outsource the manufacture of the hooks, which makes quality control difficult.

"Once you get below size 20, things just go to hell," was the way Bill Chase put it. Mustad Signature series hooks may be the one exception. Jeff Pierce of Mustad told me that Signature hooks are proportionally correct throughout all the sizes in a particular hook model.

"We studied a lot of hooks when we were designing the Signature series and realized that there was no rhyme or reason to gap size, wire diameter, or the tying length of the hooks as you go up or down in size. You'd notice that wire diameter on one hook size would increase by 7 percent and then the next size up it would increase by 16 percent and then there wouldn't be any changes for the next two sizes. In the Signature series, as you go up or down in hook size the wire diameter, hook gap, and tying length of the shank increase or decrease proportionally," Jeff said.

Nonetheless, I still expect some lack of uniformity, especially in the Japanese-made small hooks. If you feel that an absolute match in size is crucial to a fly's design (which it probably isn't), sort through the hooks in the size designation closest to what you need until you find the ones that suit your purpose.

A number of new distributors have recently entered the Japanese hook market. Although the distributors may come up with hook designs, they don't actually make them. The production of the hooks is outsourced to a limited number of manufacturers. New small-hook designs have been limited to oversize hook eyes, wide gaps, a few offset-point styles, and changes in wire color. The most popular dry-fly, nymph, and curved-shank Japanese-made small hooks are now available from several distributors, and "knocked off" versions are often indistinguishable from one another.

Major changes occurred at Partridge of Redditch when it was acquired by Mustad. The

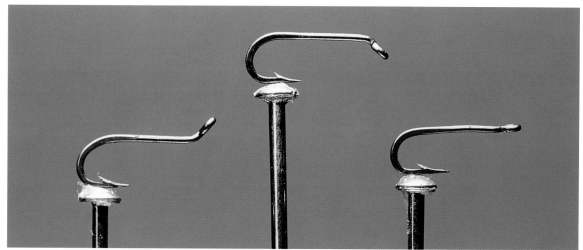

For many years Mustad "classic" hooks were the most readily available small hooks. Shown here are (left to right) the Mustad 94842 (size 22), Mustad 94840 (size 20), and Mustad 94859 (size 22). Note: The Mustad 94842 is now available only down to size 18.

Partridge hook-making machines were moved from England to Singapore, where Partridge hooks are now manufactured. Mustad continues to manufacture some of its standard (or "classic") fly hooks in its Norway facility, although most of the chemically sharpened Signature hooks are made in the Singapore facility. Mustad is one of the few hook companies that produce their own hooks without any outsourcing.

With all of this in mind, here is a list of useful small hooks.

Mustad 94840, 94842, and 94859. These are the "classic" Mustad hooks that I used for tying my first small flies. I wasn't going to include them because they incorporate some features that have fallen out of favor with small-hook designers. The most common complaints are that the points are too long and the gaps too narrow.

Many small-hook designers believe that the "effective" hook shank, which is the length of the shank measured from the spot opposite the tip of the point to the hook eye, should be equal to at least one and a half times the width of the gap. According to this theory, a hook with a shorter shank lacks the leverage to efficiently penetrate the fish's mouth. Thus, a hook with a longer point has a shorter effective shank and less hooking leverage.

If you measure any of the classic Mustad hooks, you'll find that they meet the effective-hook-shank criterion, and that the points are often *shorter* and finer than the same size hooks made by other companies. The classic Mustad hooks are also sized smaller than other brands. A size 20 Mustad standard dry-fly hook is about equal to other manufacturers' size 22 hooks. More worrisome, however, is that the gaps of the classics are narrower than other hooks.

Narrow gaps aside, I include the Mustad hooks because of a conversation I had with fly tier A. K. Best. His comment, as always, was direct. "Just think about all the trout we landed on those hooks. How many failures do you remember?"

A. K. is right. We fished the Mustad 948 series of hooks for a lot of years with fine results. They are good hooks, at a good price.

My favorite classic Mustad hooks are the turned-down eye 94840 and the straight-eye

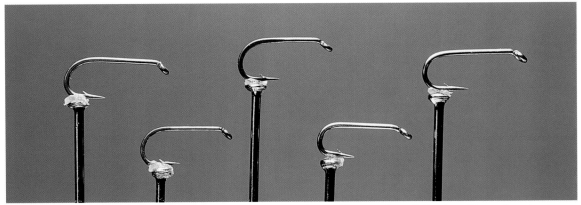

Chemically sharpened, turned-down-eye dry-fly hooks are the workhorses of small-fly tiers. Shown here in size 20 are (left to right) the Tiemco TMC 100, Mustad Signature R30 (2 Extra Fine Wire), Mustad Signature R50 (standard wire), Dai-Riki 305, and Daiichi 1100.

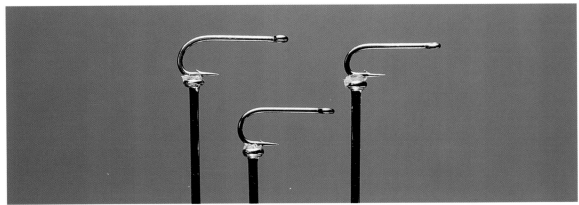

Many chemically sharpened, small dry-fly hooks are also available in straight-eye versions. Shown here in size 20 are (left to right) the Tiemco TMC 101, Daiichi 1110, and Dai-Riki 310.

94859. The Mustad 94842 is the turned-up eye version, but I've always felt that the eye is bent up at a more severe angle than necessary. All these hooks have round bends. I use these small Mustad hooks for all sorts of mayfly imitations, spent spinners, and some midge patterns.

Tiemco TMC 100, 101; Daiichi 1100, 1110; Mustad Signature R30; and Dai-Riki 305, 310. Chemically sharpened dry-fly hooks are the workhorses of small-fly tiers. They can be used for almost any pattern. All of these basic dry-fly hooks are advertised by their manufacturers as having the wide gaps favored by tiers, with

the exception of the Dai-Riki 305 (the straight-eye model 310 is Dai-Riki's wide-gap hook). Most use somewhat finer than usual wire. The Tiemco TMC 100, Daiichi 1100, Mustad R30, and Dai-Riki 305 all have turned-down eyes. The Tiemco TMC 101, Daiichi 1110, and Dai-Riki 310 are the straight-eye versions of the same hooks.

There are numerous variations of these standard dry-fly hooks available in size 18 and smaller. A few have longer shanks, many have shorter shanks, some have standard-size gaps, many are available barbless, most have round bends, one series has oversize hook eyes, there is a

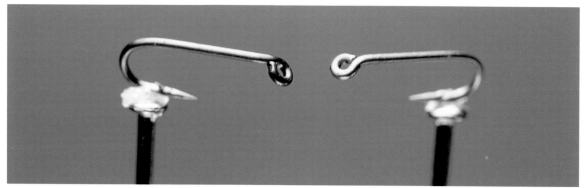

The oversize hook eye is a popular small-hook variation. Compare the size 22 Orvis "Big Eye" hook (left) and a size 22 Tiemco TMC 100 hook (right).

The Partridge K1A size 28 (left) and Tiemco TMC 518 size 28 (right).

smattering of turned-up-eye models, several feature heavier wire, and a couple come in nifty black models.

Partridge K1A and Tiemco TMC 518. The Partridge K1A is the elegant Vince Marinaro Midge Hook. It was the first hook I ever used that was designed specifically for tying small flies. It has a wide gap with an offset point, which means the point isn't exactly in line with the shank, but is bent slightly to one side. An offset point seems to help when it comes to hooking and holding a trout on a small fly. I also think it looks cool, and it gives me confidence.

The Partridge K1A has a turned-down eye and what they call a Captain Hamilton bend, but it looks round to me. The point is short, and the shank is also quite short. Some anglers say this hook straightens too easily, but you must remem-

ber it's made of 4X-fine wire. It's not the hook to use for horsing in fish. The K1A also sports a dark finish that makes for an attractive fly. I use this hook for midge emergers, midge dry flies, and stuck-in-the-shuck patterns.

The Partridge K1A was the only option in a very small, short, straight-shank hook until the Tiemco TMC 518 was introduced. The Tiemco TMC 518 has a straight eye and is made from 3X-fine wire. It doesn't have an offset point. A size 28 Partridge K1A, the smallest made, and a size 28 Tiemco TMC 518 are close to equivalent in actual size. If you feel that the offset point gives you an advantage, go with the Partridge K1A. If you prefer a little heavier wire and think that a straight eye makes for a wider effective gap, the Tiemco TMC 518 is your hook. The Tiemco TMC 518 is also available in sizes 30 and 32 if

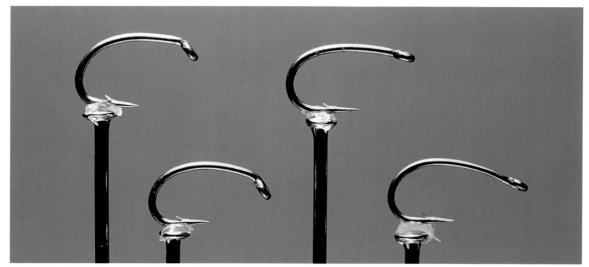

Curved-shank hooks are especially popular with small-fly tiers. Shown in size 20 are (left to right) the Daiichi 1130 (standard wire), Tiemco TMC 2487 (fine wire), Tiemco TMC 2488 (fine wire), and Mustad Signature C49S (standard wire).

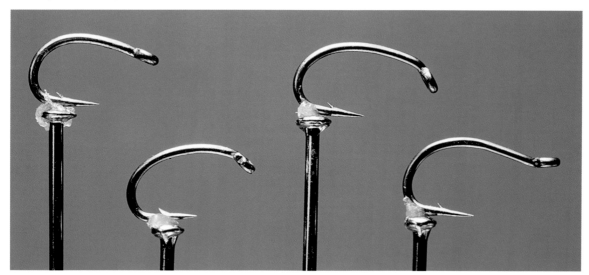

Heavy-wire curved-shank hooks include (left to right) the Tiemco TMC 2488H (size 20), Dai-Riki 135 (size 20), Tiemco TMC 2457 (size 18), and Daiichi 1150 (size 18).

you decide to get *really* small. It's the smallest hook I now use.

Daiichi 1130, 1150; Tiemco TMC 2487, TMC 2488, TMC 2488H, TMC 2457; Mustad C49S; and Dai-Riki 135, 125. These are all incarnations of the chemically sharpened,

short, continuous-bend hooks that are so popular among small-fly tiers. They are ideal for imitating midge larvae and midge pupae, and for tying floating nymphs and small scuds. They work for any patterns requiring hooks with short shanks and fairly wide gaps.

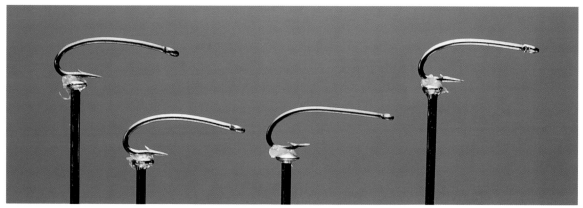

Long-shank curved hooks in small sizes have many applications. Shown here in size 20 are (left to right) the Daiichi 1270, Tiemco TMC 200R, Mustad Signature C53S, and Dai-Riki 270.

The Daiichi 1130 and Tiemco TMC 2487 have turned-down eyes and reversed points. A reversed point means that if you hold the hook right side up with the point facing you, the point will be offset to the right. The Tiemco TMC 2488, Mustad C49S, and Dai-Riki 125 all have straight eyes. The actual size of the hooks is about the same, but the curvature of the Mustad C49S hook is more pronounced. The Dai-Riki 125 is similar to the Tiemco TMC 2488. All of these hooks use finer wires.

The Daiichi 1150, Tiemco TMC 2457, Tiemco TMC 2488H, and Dai-Riki 135 are heavy-wire versions of the fine-wire hooks. The Daiichi 1150 and Tiemco TMC 2457 are available down to size 18. The Dai-Riki 135 goes down to size 22, and the Tiemco TMC 2488H goes to size 24. The heavy-wire versions of these short, curved hooks are good for tying micro-scud patterns and for any imitation that needs a touch more weight.

You should expect discrepancies in labeling among the various hook companies for these hooks. One company's "standard" wire may actually be finer than the 1X-fine designation that another company uses. A 1X-short hook in one brand may be shorter than the 2X-short hook of a different company. Another interesting observation is that none of these hooks passes the effective-shank-length formula, but they all do just fine in the field.

Tiemco TMC 200R, Daiichi 1270, Mustad C53S, and Dai-Riki 270. These are all straight-eye, 3X-long versions of curved-shank hooks. There are only minor differences among the various brand names. The Tiemco TMC 200R and Daiichi 1270 are available to size 22. The Dai-Riki 270 goes to size 24, and the Mustad C53S to size 20. These long-shank curved hooks are good for tying scuds, small aquatic annelids, and, surprisingly, curved-body dry-fly patterns.

Daiichi 1140 and Tiemco TMC 206BL. These neat little hooks both have curved shanks that flatten out more than the continuous-bend curved hooks. The hook eyes are very slightly turned up. The Tiemco TMC 206BL is barbless, black, and available to size 20. The Daiichi 1140 goes down to size 22. I like these hooks for tying midge pupae, blue-winged olive emergers, and microcaddis.

Daiichi 1480. I'm including this hook because I think it is aesthetically pleasing. It is very close to the Mustad 94859 but has a Limerick bend that just rings my chimes. Daiichi calls this a 1X-fine, 2X-short hook. It has a straight eye. I just adore it for the spent-spinner imitation I tie

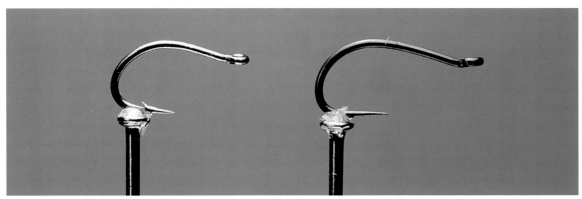

The Daiichi 1140 (left) and the Tiemco TMC 206BL (right). Both hooks are size 18.

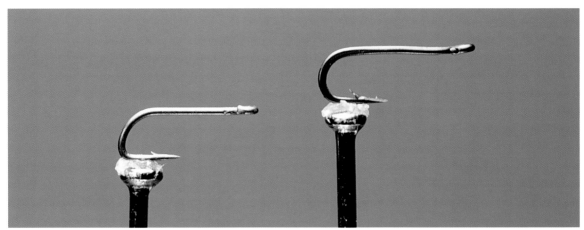

The size 24 Daiichi 1480 (left) has a unique Limerick bend. The size 24 standard Mustad 94859 (right) has the more common round bend.

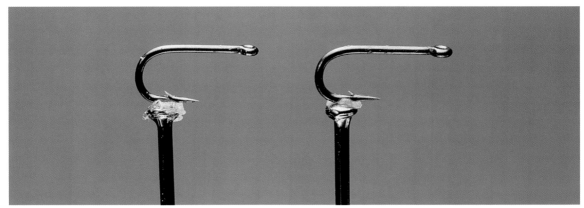

The size 20 Daiichi 1640 (left) and the size 20 Tiemco TMC 501 (right) are both short-shank hook designs made with stronger standard wire.

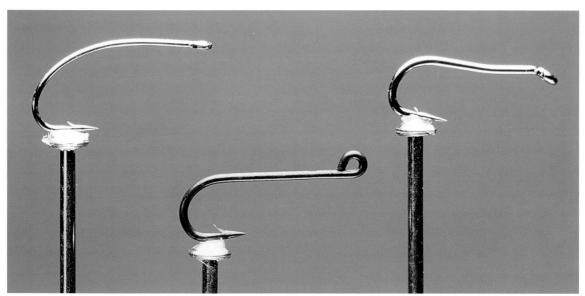

The Oliver Edwards Nymph/Emerger Partridge K14ST hook (left) and Darrel Martin's Daiichi 1220 hook (far right) are both available in silver finishes. The Davy Wotton In-Line Partridge K17 (middle) features an in-line hook eye. All three hooks are shown in size 20.

for the tiny and difficult *Baetis* spinner fall that occurs every autumn on Colorado's South Platte River.

Daiichi 1640 and Tiemco TMC 501. These similar short-shank, straight-eye hooks are made from standard-gauge wire, which means they are stronger. The Tiemco TMC 501 is 1X short with a round bend and is available in sizes 20 to 24. The Daiichi 1640 is 2X short with an offset reversed point and is available down to size 20.

Daiichi 1220, Partridge K14ST, and Partridge K17. Specialty hooks designed by well-known fly tiers always intrigue me. The Daiichi 1220 was specially designed by Darrel Martin for small dry flies. It has a Sproat bend, slightly up-turned tapered *shank,* down eye, standard wire, and slightly offset point. The most interesting feature of the hook is the upturned tapered shank, which opens the gap, reduces stress on the small hook, and cants the wing back on mayfly patterns. The hook is available in a standard bronze

finish and a silver (Crystal) finish. The silver finish makes the hook less visible to the trout.

Oliver Edwards designed the Partridge K14ST hook especially for his small nymph and emerger patterns. The straight eye and curved shank are similar to those of other long-shank curved hooks, but like Darrel Martin's Daiichi 1220 hook, this hook is finished in silver to "re-flect the colors of the subsurface world of trout and grayling." I haven't experimented with silver hooks as much as I'd like, but if Darrel Martin and Oliver Edwards believe they hold promise for small flies, I'll give them my attention.

The Partridge K17 hook is a unique design by Davy Wotton. The outstanding feature of this hook is an in-line eye. Wotton reasons that an in-line hook eye is less visible to the trout. In addi-tion, the in-line eye lends itself to midge patterns designed to hang in the surface film.

Enough. You get the idea. There are more small hooks than you'll ever need. If you stick with one company for the majority of your

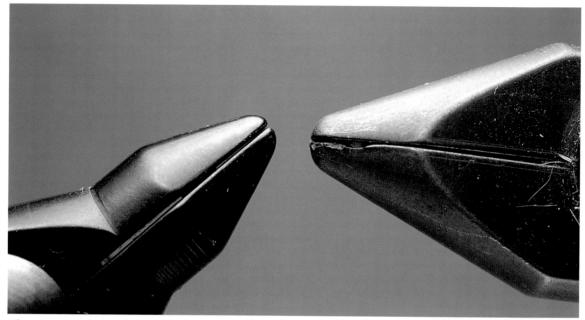

Fly-tying vises designed especially for tying small flies have a smaller, narrow "midge" jaw (left) that allows the tier to securely clamp and work with small hooks. A standard-size jaw (right) might be capable of holding a small hook, but doesn't leave enough room to tie materials to it.

small-hook needs, you'll struggle less with sizing inconsistencies among different hook brands. You can always add specific hooks from other companies as the need arises. Almost all the small hooks I've used in the last five years are excellent; I really don't see how much more they can be improved. With the increased strength of tippet material, you should be aware that some extra-fine-wire small hooks may bend under duress. The bottom line, however, is that today's manufacturers are offering a greater variety of high-quality small hooks than ever.

SMALL-FLY TYING TOOLS

There was a time when it seemed like fly tiers felt they needed small tools to tie small flies. There were tiny midge bobbins, midge hackle pliers, and specialized small-fly scissors. With a few exceptions, I always used the same tools that I used to tie standard-size flies.

The most important specialized tool you'll need to tie small flies is a vise with narrow "midge" jaws. The jaws are designed to taper to more of a point where the hook is clamped in. This makes it easier to firmly hold and work with small hooks. There are a number of companies that manufacture fly-tying vises for use with small hooks. When purchasing a small-fly tying vise, look for one that firmly holds tiny hooks and has narrow enough jaws to clamp a small hook at the bend while allowing open access to the rest of the hook for tying. A vise with a head that rotates lets you check out how the fly looks from all sides and can help when attaching materials to the hook.

I use fly-tying scissors that come to a very fine point for most of my small-fly work. In addition, I use an old fly-tying scissors solely for cutting wire and specialized surgical scissors with ultra-fine points for very exacting work. The

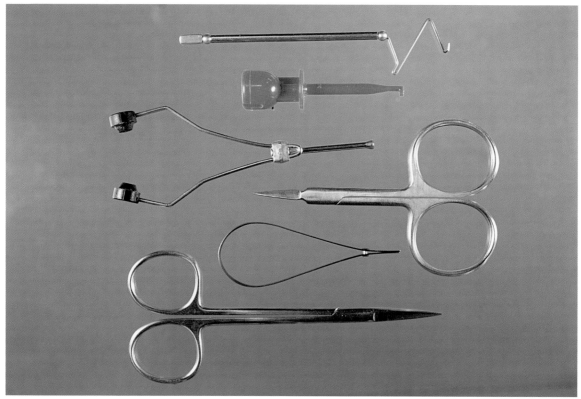

Tying small flies does not require a lot of specialized tools. From top to bottom: Tiemco Midge Whip Finish Tool, E-Z Mini-Hook Pliers, standard-size ceramic-lined thread bobbin, standard-size fly-tying scissors with fine points, J. Dorin Tear Drop Hackle Pliers, and ultra-fine-point surgical scissors.

surgical scissors, which are called iris scissors and are used for eye surgery, aren't necessary to tie a decent small fly, but I sure appreciate them when it comes to cutting out an errant hackle barb or trimming a hard-to-reach tag end of thread. The scissors are quite expensive if ordered from a medical catalog, but the rumor is that you can purchase them on the open market at a much more reasonable price.

A regular-length ceramic-tube bobbin works fine for tying small flies. Stay away from metal-tube bobbins—they will cut the fine threads required for tying small flies. I use J. Dorin Tear Drop Hackle Pliers, but any pliers that hold tiny feathers firmly will do. Spring-loaded hook pliers are useful for holding ribbing or other small ma-

terials until you can get a few wraps of thread around them. Spring-loaded hooks can also be used to wind hackle, but I find that the hackle twists when I wind it with them. I often whip-finish small flies by hand, but the Tiemco Midge Whip Finish Tool is even better.

The only factory-made mini hair stacker that I thought was suitable for small flies is no longer available. Before I bought that stacker, I got by just fine with a spent .22 caliber cartridge shell. Just put the hair into the shell tips first and gently tap it. I haven't found a commercially manufactured half-hitch tool that works well on tiny hooks, but an old, metal-tube bobbin works great.

Good light is especially important when tying small flies. You can get as picky as you want when

A factory-made hair stacker (left) with a barrel short enough for the fine, short hair used to tie tiny flies can be hard to find. A spent .22 caliber shell (right) works fine in a pinch.

it comes to how you illuminate your work area, but I keep it pretty simple. My only requirement is that I like the light to come from two directions because I think it gives me better depth perception. At home I use a 100-watt incandescent lamp and a fluorescent lamp. A contrast card placed behind the vise will also help you see the fly.

There are two types of magnifiers available for small-fly tiers. The most popular magnifier is mounted on a gooseneck and attached to the vise. Others are incorporated into an unattached adjustable lamp. The lens of either one is placed between the tier and the fly, where it can be adjusted to the proper distance to clearly magnify the fly. Some tiers believe that a rimless magnifier causes less eye strain. The advantage of the lens-type magnifier is that it's easy to move away from the fly when not needed and gives sharp, clear magnification. The disadvantage is that the magnifier limits the working space your hands have around the vise. Other magnifiers, such as jewelers' magnifiers, are worn around the head and can be flipped over the eyes when needed. They are easy to use, but the neck and shoulders may get tired holding them in focus. Some tiers have an optometrist make them eyeglasses with a particular magnification for their small-fly tying needs.

More than anything, I've found that the fewer gizmos and gadgets I have cluttering my fly-tying desk, the more I can concentrate on the work at hand. I like it that way.

CHAPTER THREE

Hanging by a Thread

It all started with a simple statement. A fellow small-fly tier told me that one brand of thread labeled 8/0 was the same as another brand that carries a 14/0 designation. As it turned out, the two threads he mentioned were the only two I'd ever used to tie size 20 and smaller flies because they were the only brands my local fly shop carried in sizes for small flies.

My friend was adamant that the two threads were identical, but I *knew* that they didn't tie the same. They might be the same in some technical, measurable sense, but I could tell the difference when I tied flies. The thread sold as 14/0 let me sneak in an extra wrap here and there without increasing the bulk of a fly.

Those of us who tie small flies are always concerned with bulk. If anything, tying small flies is fly tying stripped to its most basic elements. It's not difficult. There's seldom more than three or four steps involving two or three materials. The trick is to maintain proportions and as slim a profile as possible. Thread, one of the most basic considerations in fly tying, is a real factor. I wondered why I'd never experimented with different brands of finer threads or even seriously considered the impact they could have when tying small flies.

Fly-tying threads suitable for small flies come in a huge variety of colors and diameters. Each one has its own characteristics. It pays to test many threads to find those most suited to your style and needs.

I decided to get hold of as many different small-fly threads as I could to see if I noticed differences among them. That's how I entered into the secret world of fly-tying thread obsession, thread fanaticism, and thread heresy. It was the path of the thread head.

As it turns out, I was not the first to wonder about fly-tying thread. Chris Helm and Bill Merg did an exhaustive comparison of fly-tying threads

The "ought" system of describing threads really doesn't tell you much. All of these threads look alike, but the three on the left are sold as 8/0 and the one on the right, which appears slightly finer, is actually sold as 6/0. Depending on its composition, each thread will also produce a different thickness when wrapped around the hook shank. The lesson? Tying with a thread is the only way to know anything about it.

that took more than a year to complete. The results of their work appeared in the Summer 1996 issue of *Fly Tyer* magazine.

An obvious lesson of Helm and Merg's work was that the "ought" system of designating thread diameter—3/0, 6/0, 8/0, and so on—is totally arbitrary. Although most fly tiers assume that the higher the ought number the smaller the diameter of thread, that is not always the case. Merg measured thread diameters and came up with some startling facts, such as that Danville's Flymaster 6/0 thread has a *smaller* diameter than Gordon Griffith's 14/0 thread. Threads with the same ought designation varied a lot in actual diameter, as measured by Merg.

Diameter seemed a logical place to start in a study of threads suitable for tying small flies. I went through the Merg test chart and marked off the thinnest threads in 6/0, 8/0, 10/0, 12/0, and 14/0. The plan was to get samples of as many of these threads as possible to test.

I wasn't as interested in a quantitative appraisal of the thread, such as the work Merg and Helm had done, as I was in a qualitative, subjective examination. I wanted to know how the thread felt in the hand, how easy it was to bind materials down with it, how it flattened to reduce bulk, how it tied off at the head, and how it held dubbing. I figured I was well suited to do a qualitative test because I'm no fly-tying wizard. I get just as frustrated tying a "hard" fly as anyone. Simply put, I'm your everyman fly tier. One of the reasons I like small flies is because they catch fish where I live and they are easy to tie. I'm a fly-fishing guide who has to use small flies. I tie them to catch fish. I want them to be relatively easy to tie and durable. If I can manage to make my flies look nice in the process, I'm a happy camper.

THREAD TESTS

With that in mind I decided on a simple test. I would tie a size 22 Flashback Pheasant Tail with each thread sample, and then jot down what I

On small flies, thread makes a big difference. Note the difference in bulk between these partially tied size 22 Flashback Pheasant Tails. The thread on the left is Gudebrod 10/0; on the right is Benecchi 8/0.

The effect of thread is even more apparent on the finished nymphs. The fly tied with the thicker thread is noticeably fatter.

thought about each thread when I finished the fly. I chose the Flashback Pheasant Tail because it has a number of steps utilizing a number of materials. I'd have to bind down the fine copper ribbing. At the rear of the thorax I'd have to tie in the Mylar flashback material and then tie in the peacock herl. That's a fair amount of tying in a small area on a tiny fly. It would be a good test of how bulky a thread was. The same would apply at the head of the fly, where I'd have to tie down the peacock herl, the wing case, and the Mylar, and then form a head. There was an ulterior motive, too—I use a lot of size 22 Flashback Pheasant Tails. I'd be able to put the samples in my fly box for the ultimate test.

The dubbing test would be more straightforward. I would simply dub a wisp of beaver on each thread and see how well it "stuck." Then I'd throw a few wraps around the hook shank to see if the dubbing stayed on the thread when I wound it. Plain and simple. I chose beaver because I use it on a lot of small-fly patterns and am familair with its dubbing characteristics.

I decided on a simple three-star rating system for dubbing. One star was below average, meaning it was difficult to dub the beaver onto the thread, that the dubbing came off when wrapped around the hook, or both. Two stars meant the thread dubbed well in all ways and I had no complaints. Three stars would mean the thread accepted dubbing exceptionally well.

I started contacting thread manufacturers and distributors. When I was done I had a dozen threads to test—Gudebrod 10/0, Gudebrod 8/0, Benecchi 12/0, Benecchi 10/0, Benecchi 8/0, Wapsi 70-denier Ultra Thread, Danville's Flymaster waxed 6/0, Danville's Flymaster unwaxed 6/0, Gordon Griffith's Sheer 14/0, Gordon Griffith's Wisp 8/0, Gordon Griffith's Cobweb 6/0, and Uni-thread 8/0.

THREAD COMPOSITION

While waiting for the samples to arrive, I reviewed what the distributors had told me and educated myself on the fine points of tying threads. Danville's Flymaster 6/0 and Wapsi's Ultra Thread are nylon. All the other threads I'd be testing are made of polyester. All but one of the threads has a simple-twist construction,

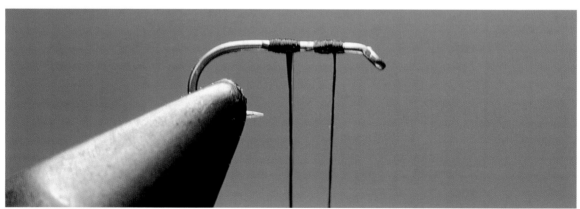

How much a thread flattens has a lot to do with how much bulk it creates. The number of twists per inch of the thread is a factor. Some threads, such as the Gordon Griffith's Sheer 14/0 on the right, resist flattening because they have more twists per inch, while others, such as the 70-denier Ultra Thread on the left, spread out and flatten very easily because they have fewer twists per inch. Inexperienced tiers, however, might find that floss-like, flat threads are easier to fray and slightly harder to manage.

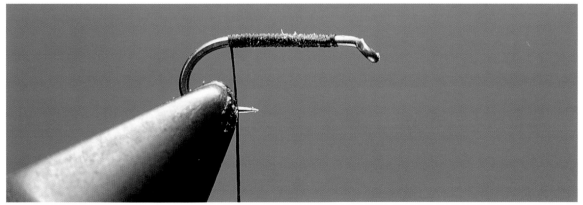

Size 8/0 Uni-thread is "semibonded," which means the fibers are in effect glued together. It makes the thread more cordlike, an ideal property when making thread-body midge imitations.

Note how the body of the finished midge imitation tied with the semibonded thread appears segmented.

which means the fibers are twisted into a single strand. The Gordon Griffith's Cobweb thread has a rope-twist construction in which two single strands are twisted together.

The simple-twist threads differ in the degree of twist each one has. A thread with more twists per inch is less likely to flatten on the hook; it adds more bulk than does a thread with fewer twists. But a thread with fewer twists is more prone to fraying.

One thread, the 8/0 Uni-thread, is semibonded, which means its fibers are glued together to prevent it from flattening. Most of the threads I examined are lightly waxed. The wax might

make them a bit stronger by binding the fibers together, although thread strength isn't crucial when tying small flies because you rarely have to put much pressure on materials.

Only one company, Wapsi, uses the denier system to describe its thread. The denier is a textile industry standard. It's defined as a unit of fineness for silk, rayon, or nylon yarns based on a standard of 50 milligrams per 450 meters of yarn—just in case you ever want to weigh out your threads. What's nice about the denier system is that it creates a relative scale based on a real standard. You know, for instance, that a 70-denier thread is twice as fine as a 140-denier thread. Of

All of the threads tested were easy to apply dubbing to. The key, of course, is to use just a wisp of material.

course, the denier number doesn't tell you how a thread will flatten when wrapped on a hook or anything about its construction. Bill Merg recommended a complete system for classifying fly-tying threads in the Summer 1998 issue of *Fly Tyer,* but even just a denier rating would be an improvement over the "ought" system.

So, with all of this in mind, here are my notes, thoughts, and a few recommendations on the threads I tested for small-fly tying. I should note that the dubbing test was a bit of a wash because *all* the threads dubbed well as far as I was concerned. If you see a plus sign by the star rating it's because I thought the dubbing qualities of a thread were a little better than the stars I gave. You'll notice that I didn't consider the strength of any of the threads. I was prepared to note if any of the threads broke while tying the flies, but none did. Unlike spinning deer hair, tying small flies requires a light touch. All the threads tested were strong enough for the task.

NOTES ON A DOZEN THREADS

Gudebrod 10/0: The thread is silky to the touch and lies very flat. It makes binding the materials to the hook a breeze. It's "flossy" in nature and has a very slight tendency to fray. It's a slick thread that can slide down over the eye of the hook when tying the head off, but just a little vigilance prevents that. It makes a beautiful head on a small fly. Chris Helm said that if you applied the "ought" system to this thread's diameter (as Bill Merg tested them) it would be an honest 16/0. It's a true midge thread, wonderful to tie with. My life is changed. Dubbing score: ***

Gordon Griffith's 14/0 Sheer: This thread is my old friend. It tends more toward a "cord" than a floss. It takes a bit more concentration to bind materials down, but after a few wraps it's fine. There were some tiny flakes of white stuff on the thread that were distracting. I assume they were little bits of wax. I attached the Mylar for the flashback with three wraps and it pulled out when I went to bring it over the top of the wing case. You just need to crank down a little harder on this thread when binding materials. The diameter of the thread is quite fine. You will feel good about winding a few extra wraps with it. It's an excellent thread for tying small flies. Dubbing score: **+

Benecchi 12/0: This thread flattens nicely. You can tell that when binding down the wire for the rib. It grabs the wire well with just a wrap or two and holds it firmly. In fact, it binds all materials well. This thread must have a few more twists—it's more cordlike, with no tendency to fray when whip-finishing the head, which is something I notice because I often tie off my flies by hand, without a tool. A perfectly serviceable small-fly thread. Dubbing score: ***

Benecchi 10/0: The characteristics of this thread are very similar to those of the 12/0, but it is definitely heavier. That shows up when binding down the materials at the rear of the thorax and at the head of the Flashback Pheasant Tail. You don't feel safe putting that extra wrap around the materials if you are trying to keep the bulk down. Dubbing score: **

Wapsi 70-Denier Ultra Thread: This is a very flossy thread. The beauty of this is that Ultra Thread binds down materials wonderfully. The drawback is that it frays more easily. This is a problem for me when I whip-finish the head of the fly by hand. It would probably be better to use a whip-finishing tool with this thread. Tom Schmuecker at Wapsi says Ultra Thread has only three to four twists per inch, which means it's almost a simple multifilament thread. It sure flattens great. I don't feel bad about whipping an extra security wrap or two around any of the materials because it flattens to almost nothing. If you like the Gudebrod 10/0, this thread is even flossier. Dubbing score: **

Gordon Griffith's 6/0 Cobweb: This is a pretty heavy thread, though I could still tie a size 22 fly with it. It binds materials well, but it's right at the limit for a fly this size when it comes to bulk. Although I initially thought all the threads in my test were simple twists, this one actually looks like it could be a rope twist in which two strands of thread are twisted together. Sometimes those two strands will separate and unravel. Not a bad thread, but you may want to reserve it for larger hook sizes. Dubbing score: **

Gordon Griffith's 8/0 Wisp: This is the quintessential middle-of-the-road thread. It flattens nicely, but not too much. The bulk factor is manageable. It is silky to the touch and actually a bit stiff, which I take to mean there is a fair amount of wax on it. As on the Griffith's 14/0 Sheer, there is the occasional white fleck of what appears to be wax on the thread. It doesn't seem to affect the tying qualities of the thread. An all-around decent thread for small flies. Dubbing score: **+

Danville's Flymaster 6/0 (waxed): This was the big surprise. It ties like a 10/0 thread. It's silky to the touch, flattens almost like the flossier threads, and binds materials beautifully. It doesn't give the sensation that it wants to roll the materials when you bind them down. This may be because Flymaster is nylon rather than polyester. Whatever it is, I like it a lot for small flies. This thread has been around forever, but I overlooked it when I got into tying small flies. I won't do that from now on. Laura Farley at Danville says that it's probably closer to a 7/0, but it's been called a 6/0 for so many years the company just decided to keep the designation the same. Dubbing score: ***

Danville's Flymaster 6/0 (unwaxed): There is little discernible difference to me between this thread and the waxed Flymaster. It feels a bit less slick. I'd pick the waxed version over this, but it is quite close. Dubbing score: **

Uni-thread 8/0: This thread binds materials and flattens down amazingly well. I thought a bonded thread wasn't supposed to flatten—if it doesn't, it sure packs down nicely. It has a tendency to roll the material slightly on the first wrap or two. It's a bit bulky, but that may be because it's an honest 8/0 thread. This thread is bonded, which makes it a great choice for making the thread bodies so common on many small flies. Dubbing score: **+

Benecchi 8/0: The Benecchi 8/0 is much bulkier than I expected. It's marginally suited for a size 22 hook in my estimation. It was difficult to get in the necessary wraps to tie off the head of the fly, but the thread does flatten nicely. I'd stick to the Benecchi 12/0 or the 10/0 for small flies. Dubbing score: **

Gudebrod 8/0: Like the Gudebrod 10/0, this is a flossier type of thread. It flattens nicely, but is a bit bulky for small flies. It doesn't tend to fray too much, which is nice. It is serviceable for small flies, but is beginning to push the limit for an 8/0 thread. Dubbing score: ***

There you have it. If I've learned anything, it's that judging a tying thread for small flies is a very subjective business. It comes down to what you are trying to achieve and, more simply, what you like. I found that I like a thread that binds materials firmly and feels a bit slick. My three favorites were the Gudebrod 10/0, the waxed Flymaster 6/0, and the Benecchi 12/0, but the Gordon Griffith's 14/0 and the Uni-thread 8/0 were virtually tied with the Benecchi. The big surprises for me were the Flymaster and that old standby, the Uni 8/0.

The point is, you owe it to yourself to test these threads. You may not agree with me, but you may find a thread that really works for you.

It's easy to think that tying thread is just tying thread, but I used to think that hackle was just hackle until I discovered some genetic varieties that wound better than anything I'd ever experienced. The fact is that the right materials, tools, and thread will make it easier for you to tie better-looking small flies even if your skill level remains the same. Chris Helm, who is a fly-tying wizard, put it right when he said, "It's amazing how many fly tiers don't consider thread important. They figure thread is thread, but that's like saying all you need to play golf is a nine iron."

Indeed. After these tests, I'm a thread head, too.

CHAPTER FOUR

A Little Flash

When a nymph starts to hatch, the abdomen of the dun is partially withdrawn, so that a space appears between the tail end of the dun's body and the tail end of the nymphal shuck, and this space becomes filled with the gas. The tail end of the hatching nymph then immediately assumes a much increased lustre, and in fact it strongly resembles a section of glass tube which has been filled with mercury.

This effect is even more noticeable in the pupae of those long-legged midges, the chironomids when they are hatching at the surface of the open water of lakes, and I think that it explains the added attraction which a flat tag of gold or silver gives to many artificial flies.

— J. R. Harris, *An Angler's Entomology* (1956)

Stocking and maintaining an aquarium of aquatic insects used to be part of everyone's angling apprenticeship. I remember going dutifully to my home river, Colorado's South Platte, and collecting a few stones, some silt, and gravel, and then arranging them in an aerated ten-gallon aquarium. I didn't really expect much, which made it even more of a surprise when I witnessed a grand hatch of midges followed by a grander hatch of Tricos and a smattering of pale morning duns. The Trico hatch was prolific enough that I even had a little mating swarm of them near the ceiling of my study.

Other than the sheer joy of seeing aquatic insects emerge closeup, I actually did learn something from the aquarium experience. I found out that midge pupae often swim up to the water's surface, momentarily hang vertically, then swim back down about six inches. They typically repeat this cycle several times more before lying horizontally in the surface film and hatching.

I discovered later that the pupae gather a little bit of air each time they make the trip to the surface, and that this air is used to inflate their pupal shuck. And that shuck does indeed look like a "glass tube filled with mercury." It's uncanny how flashy they are. The same held true, to a slightly lesser degree, for the Trico nymphs. These are lessons I have never forgotten.

Tying small flies constantly teaches me what makes a trout take one fly and ignore another. Adding a little flash to a pattern is the most consistent "trigger" that I have found. I'm not the only fly tier who has picked up this trick, either. Whether you use coarse hare's-mask fibers to catch a flashy bubble of air, or add a bright silver rib, or tie a Mylar flashback, the point is always the same. Trout respond to flash.

Long before Harris made his observations, fly fishers knew that adding a little sparkle increases the effectiveness of a fly pattern. It's difficult to determine when fly tiers first incorporated flash into fly patterns, but the use of gold wires and silk as ribs dates back to the early history of European fly tying. In America, Theodore Gordon talked enthusiastically about seeking out old

Various vinyl materials, both tubular and solid, are used to form shiny, translucent abdomens on midge patterns. Peacock herl or dubbing makes a good thorax.

San Juan Midge Emergers demonstrate the use of flashy materials on small flies. From left to right: the original pattern with a silver rib; one with a short Antron wing; a San Juan Emerger with two strands of Krystal Flash for the wing; and another variation with a small glass bead at the head.

epaulets from military uniforms because the fine gold thread made excellent rib material.

It's equally difficult to determine why early fly tiers used the materials. The odds are that they used ribs to make their flies more durable. It could also be that the flashy ribbing materials were used simply because they were available. Maybe the tiers thought a little flash just made their patterns look more attractive. Whatever the reason, fly fishers began to believe that a little flash attracts the trout.

SYNTHETIC MATERIALS ADD MORE FLASH

The real revolution in small-fly flash occurred with the advent of synthetic materials in fly design. Small-fly tiers found that materials such as Antron, polypropylene, Mylar, clear and colored tubular PVC materials, glass beads, and brass beads were well suited for use in small flies. The synthetic materials added tremendous flash to small-fly patterns with little additional bulk.

The evolution of the use of flashy synthetics in small flies can be traced through the development of the popular San Juan Midge Emerger that was introduced on the San Juan River in northwestern New Mexico. The fly was tied to represent midge pupae found in autopsied or pumped stomach samples of the river's trout. The pattern, like all good small flies, was simple and to the point. The fly was initially tied on small, standard, dry-fly hooks, but later renditions were made on curved-shank Tiemco TMC 2487 or 200R hooks. The abdomen was black thread ribbed with fine silver or gold wire. The exaggerated thorax was black beaver dubbing. The pattern was a good imitation of the midge pupa found in the stomach samples.

With the advent of flashy synthetic materials, tiers began to add a short wing of white Antron or a related synthetic. The wing either extends from the rear of the thorax or is tied in at the head. This simple addition increased the effectiveness of the pattern. It took the San Juan Emerger from a simple rendition of what appeared in stomach samples to an accurate imitation of an *emerging* midge pupa. The added flash of the wing was an attempt, whether preconceived or created by chance, at imitating the "lustre" that Harris so aptly described in his observations of emerging pupae. Other renditions of this concept included the use of one or two short strands of Krystal Flash or a similar material.

The latest San Juan Midge Emerger is tied with a clear glass bead at the head of the fly (most tiers delete the short wing on this pattern). Glass-bead midge and small mayfly emergers are currently the rage on western tailwaters. In some locations they are affectionately known as "trout candy." The color of the beads runs the gamut, but clear glass seems to be the most popular. The glass beads have mainly been used as an addition to established patterns such as the Brassie, Pheasant Tail, Gold-Ribbed Hare's Ear, thread patterns, quill- and biot-body imitations, and dubbed-body standards, but that is changing as fly tiers experiment with new ideas. Beads are available at hobby stores and craft shops, but smaller, more uniform glass beads are sold by the larger fly-tying materials suppliers.

A TINY FLASHBACK PHEASANT TAIL

Hook: Regular dry-fly or nymph hook, size 20.
Thread: Brown 8/0 to 14/0.
Tail: The tips of four pheasant-tail fibers.
Abdomen: Pheasant-tail fibers.
Back: Flat Mylar tinsel.
Rib: Fine copper wire.
Thorax: Peacock herl.
Wing case: Pheasant-tail fibers and flat Mylar tinsel.
Legs: Pheasant-tail fibers.

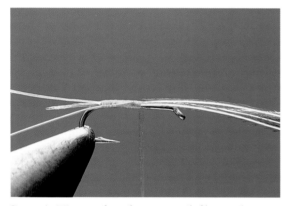

Step 1. Tie on the pheasant-tail fiber tails, copper wire, and Mylar tinsel and wrap the tying thread to the middle of the hook.

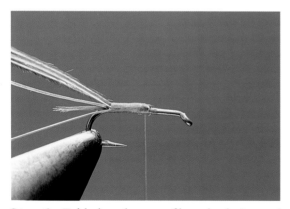

Step 2. Fold the pheasant fibers back (toward the tail), wrap the thread back over them and then wrap it forward to the middle of the hook.

Step 3. Wind the pheasant fibers forward to form the abdomen. Tie them off.

Step 4. Pull the Mylar over the top of the abdomen and tie it down.

Step 5. Wind the wire rib and tie it off.

Step 6. Tie in the herl and wrap the thorax.

Step 8. Brush back two pheasant fibers on each side of the head, clip the rest, and then form the head.

Step 7. Pull the pheasant fibers over the thorax to form the wing case. Pull the Mylar forward over the wing case.

Step 9. Clip the legs to length.

Disco midges have slim, bright bodies made of Krystal Flash or a similar material. Thoraxes are peacock herl, dubbing, or glass beads—or omitted altogether.

Mylar products also add flash to small flies. The Flashback versions of the Pheasant Tail and Gold-Ribbed Hare's Ear nymphs are good examples. Pearlescent Mylar was originally used to make only wing cases on these flies, but most recently this material is used to cover the entire backs of these nymphs.

It was only a matter of time before synthetic materials became the major component of small flies. An entire genre of patterns, often referred to as Disco flies, has a thin abdomen made entirely of Krystal Flash and an optional thorax of peacock herl or dubbing. When tied on curved-shank hooks, such as Tiemco's TMC 2487 or 200R, these patterns are good imitations of midge pupae or nymphs. The red version of this pattern is a popular representation of certain chironomid larvae found in tailwaters and spring creeks, but other colors are also effective. Where I live in Colorado, a blue Disco-type midge is par-

ticularly effective during the winter months. It's important to note that the lighter Mylar materials—especially pearlescent—change color tones depending on the color of thread used to tie the fly. Mylar is slightly translucent, and you should experiment with different colors of thread for wrapping underbodies.

My experience with Disco midge patterns varies. Very bright, light colored, flashy patterns can be quite effective at certain times of the year but don't have the year-round effectiveness of the red Disco midge on western tailwaters. My preference still tends toward patterns with a somewhat more subdued use of the flashy materials. This more subdued effect can be obtained by adding a Mylar rib around a body made from goose or turkey biot. The Mylar rib fits nicely between the ridges of the wrapped biot, adding substantial flash to the pattern.

MYLAR-RIBBED BIOT MIDGE

Hook: TMC 100 or similar dry-fly hook, sizes 18 to 22.
Thread: Black Gudebrod 10/0.
Body: Goose biot, color to match natural.
Thorax: Black Umpqua Superfine dubbing.
Rib: Pearlescent Krystal Flash.

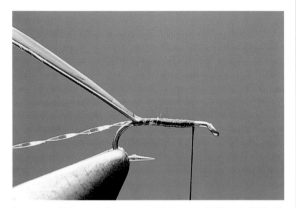

Step 1. Tie on the goose biot and Krystal Flash rib.

Step 3. Wrap the Krystal Flash rib forward in the spaces between the rough rib and tie it off.

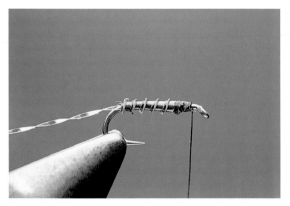

Step 2. Wind the goose biot forward so that the rough rib is up and tie it off. (Note: If you wind the biot one way and it comes out smooth, simply turn it around so that the other edge is facing forward and it will come out with the rough rib out. For the "notch" method of determining whether the biot comes out smooth or rough, see chapter 10.)

Step 4. Dub the thorax, form the head, and whip-finish the thread.

Jim Auman, a gifted Colorado guide, ties a very simple, black-thread midge imitation that uses synthetic material in a unique way. He was given the pattern by Denver area resident Jay Core. The fly is essentially a thread midge pattern with pearlescent Krystal Flash "breathers" on either side of the thorax. The hint of flash on the sides of the thorax is enough to get the trout's attention.

MIDGE EMERGER

Hook: TMC 100, TMC 101, size 20 or 22.
Thread: Black Gudebrod 10/0.
Abdomen: Black Gudebrod 10/0 thread.
Thorax: Black Gudebrod 10/0 thread.
Wings: Two strands of pearlescent Krystal Flash.

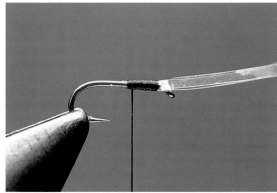

Step 1. Tie in two strands of Krystal Flash at the head of the fly with the ends pointed over the eye of the hook. Wrap the thread over the ends to build up the thorax.

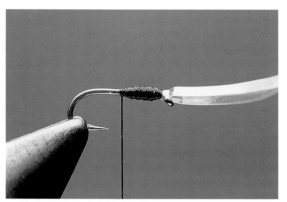

Step 2. Continue to build up the thorax.

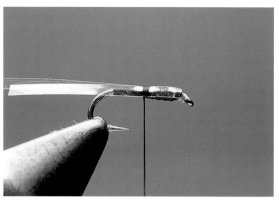

Step 4. Pull the Krystal Flash back to the rear of the thorax and tie off.

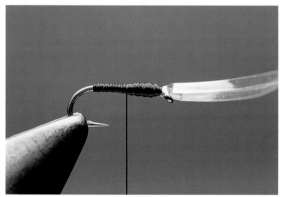

Step 3. When the thorax is complete, wrap the thread to the hook bend and back to form a thin abdomen.

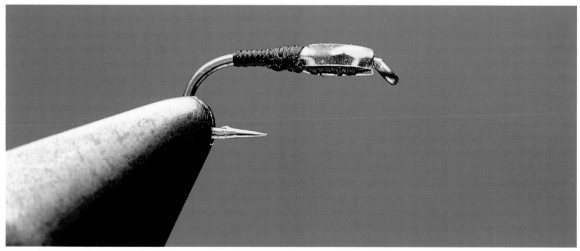

Step 5. Trim the Krystal Flash and whip-finish at the rear of the thorax.

Another Auman midge pattern, the Benacle, uses two flashy materials in an interesting way. A rib of pearlescent Krystal Flash is wrapped forward over a thread body and then a fine copper wire rib is reverse wrapped over the Krystal Flash. The thread body keeps the silhouette slim and the two ribs create enough flash to trigger the trout's feeding instincts.

BENACLE

Hook: TMC 100, TMC 101, size 20 or 22.
Thread: Black Gudebrod 10/0.
Body: Black Gudebrod 10/0 thread.
Rib 1:   Pearlescent Krystal Flash, one strand.
Rib 2:   Fine copper wire.

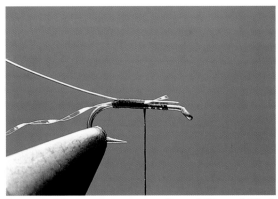

Step 1. Tie on the copper rib and Krystal Flash rib and then form a slender thread body by winding the thread forward and then back to the rear of the fly.

Step 2. With the thread at the rear of the body, make a helical wind forward to form an invisible rib.

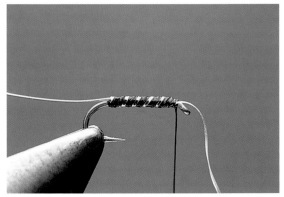

Step 3. Wrap the Krystal Flash rib forward, butting it up against the thread rib to prevent slipping.

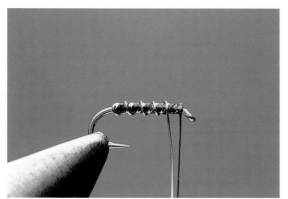

Step 4. Wind the copper rib forward in the reverse direction of the Krystal Flash rib.

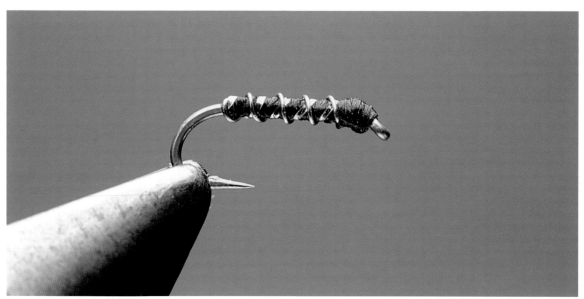

Step 5. Tie off the rib. Form a head and whip-finish.

Craig Mathew's Sparkle Dun is used as a flashy trailing shuck of Z-Lon.

Synthetic materials are also used to add a touch of flash to small flies designed to float on the surface or in the surface film. Antron and Z-Lon are used as trailing shucks. Craig Mathews's Sparkle Dun, a required pattern for tailwater and spring-creek anglers, is essentially a Compara-dun with a trailing shuck made of Z-Lon. Various "stuck-in-the-shuck" patterns are made using Z-Lon to represent wings trapped in the pupal or nymphal shuck.

Synthetic materials have revolutionized the way small flies are tied. Perhaps the trout mistake these patterns for the gas-filled shucks of emerging nymphs and pupae, or maybe glittery little flies work simply because they are more visible. One thing is for sure: The trout like them.

That's enough for me.

CHAPTER FIVE

Wired

Fine wire has long been an indispensable fly-tying material. Fly tiers initially used wire to make ribs on dubbed bodies, and wire is still the perfect material for imitating the abdominal segmentation of aquatic insects. When nymphs came into vogue, tiers began wrapping wire around hook shanks under the dubbing to weight their flies.

Frank Sawyer took fly tying with wire to a new level when he created the Pheasant Tail Nymph. Sawyer wanted an imitation that would sink when he was sight-fishing to nymphing trout. As I understand the story, he substituted copper wire for tying thread. The thorax of the original Pheasant Tail Nymph was exposed copper wire, which gave the fly a little flash. In a sense, the original Pheasant Tail Nymph was a precursor of today's flashy beadhead nymphs.

On the South Platte River in Colorado, Gene Lynch, Ken Chandler, and Tug Davenport collaborated to create the South Platte Brassie. Tying the Brassie is the epitome of simplicity: wrap copper wire around the hook shank and add a peacock-herl collar or a large thread head if you feel like it. The Brassie has been tied on small hooks since its birth in the 1960s. The copper

wire simulates the abdominal segmentation of the midge or caddisfly larvae and pupae common in the South Platte, and also adds weight to the fly.

The Brassie can be fished deep using dead-drift nymphing tactics. Beyond helping this small fly to sink, the copper wire gives the fly a touch of flash. This flash depicts the glint often associated with emerging pupae when their shucks fill with gases.

THE WIRE BUSINESS

When I first started tying Brassies in the 1970s, the standard admonition was that you must tie only a few at a time. Tiers who cranked out a season's supply over the winter found that the bright, shiny copper oxidized within a month or so, and the flies became ineffective. At that time we stripped our copper wire out of the insulation of old extension cords or telephone cords because it was about the right gauge for sizes 18 to 22 hooks.

As the word got around about the effectiveness of the Brassie, innovative tiers began using enameled wire stripped from old motor armatures and transformers. The most common colors

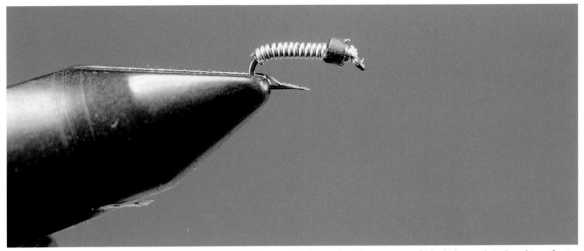

The original Brassie tied in the 1960s has a copper-wire body and a short piece of black heat-shrink tubing for its head. The author borrowed the fly from Bill Chandler, whose father, Ken, was one of the inventors of the Brassie.

were red and green. The red wire in particular was quite effective in imitating the red chironomids, known as blood worms, that are common in many rivers.

I eventually tired of stripping perfectly serviceable telephone cords and began buying spooled wire at the local fly shop. That's when I made an interesting discovery: The fly-shop copper wire didn't oxidize. It stayed as bright as it was the day I bought it.

That discovery led me to Bill Chandler, CEO of Electro-Mech in Colorado Springs and the son of Brassie co-inventor Ken Chandler. Electro-Mech makes electric motors and they use a *lot* of copper wire. I began by asking Bill to tell me the real story about the invention of the Brassie. According to legend, the Brassie came about as an accident when copper wire which was being used to weight a standard dubbed nymph imitation somehow came off, exposing the copper. The trout loved it and the Brassie was born.

"You know, I don't really know how they came up with that fly," Bill said.

That crushed my hopes of ever finding out the real story of the Brassie, but Bill gave me the impression that the pattern may not have been the result of an accident. He did say the Brassie became so popular in the 1960s that his father and the other fly fishers in their group actually marketed it. The flies had the well-known copper-wire body with a black head of heat-shrink tubing. Each fly was placed in a clear gelatin capsule and displayed on a card.

"I don't know how it works, but those Brassies in the gelatin capsules are as bright today as the day we made them in the 1960s," Bill said.

According to Bill, the copper wire I bought at the fly shop was coated with a clear polyurethane and a nylon overcoat—that's why it doesn't oxidize. The coating is only .001 inch thick on the smaller gauges of wire. "Magnet wire," as it's known in the electric-motor industry, is available in an almost infinite variety of gauges, giving fly tiers the opportunity to vary the weight of their Brassies.

I brought a bag full of different spools of "fly shop" wire for Bill to examine. Most fly tiers are aware that different colors of wire have recently appeared in many fly shops. Bill was familiar with the red and green wires.

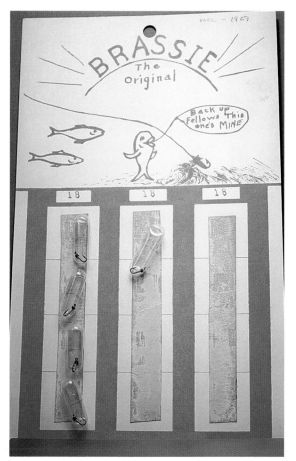 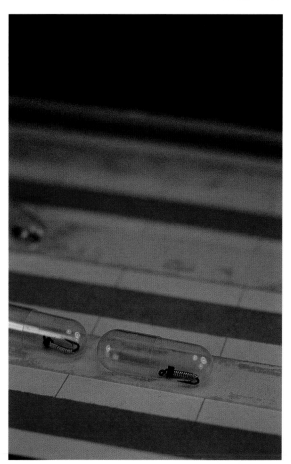

Brassies sold in the 1960s were packaged in gelatin capsules to keep the copper wire from oxidizing. Forty-odd years later, the flies look as good as new.

"We use the red and green colors in the industry so we can identify the various windings on a motor. It's still copper wire, but a dye has been added to the coating to get the color," Bill said.

I showed him spools of silver wire and gold wire. He determined that the gold wire was actually insulated copper with a dye used to create the color. The silver wire was uninsulated copper wire that had been plated to get the color. The recent availability of the dyed copper wire in a variety of colors has brought about a whole new generation of Brassies.

USING COLORED WIRE TO CREATE TWO-TONE FLIES

Rick Murphy, an innovative fly tier and respected guide on the South Platte River, has been working with the various combinations of colored wire to produce two-tone Brassies. The flies have proved quite effective on the South Platte River. Murphy uses Tiemco TMC 100, 200R, or 2487 hooks in sizes 18 to 24 for his two-wire Brassies. The wires are tied in behind the hook eye and overwrapped evenly to the end of the shank to produce a smooth underbody. Murphy then carefully separates the two wires so they don't twist

The shiny copper wire used in the original Brassies now comes in a variety of colors. It is coated with clear polyurethane and a nylon overcoat to prevent oxidation. Dye added to the polyurethane results in wires of different colors.

together, holding one strand on each side of the hook. The two wires are then held together and wound forward. Once the first wrap or two is made, the wire lays down smoothly with alternating colors. Effective color combinations include black and copper, red and silver, and green and copper. Murphy ties a small wing of white Saap Body Fur, which is similar to Z-Lon and other bright synthetics, at the head of the fly to add a little extra flash. A peacock-herl collar completes the fly.

MURPHY'S TWO-WIRE BRASSIE

Hook: TMC 200R, TMC 2487, TMC 100, sizes 18 to 24.
Thread: Black 8/0 to 14/0.
Abdomen: Two different colors of fine copper wire.
Wing: Saap Body Fur or similar synthetic material.
Thorax: Peacock herl.

Step 3. Tie in a sparse wing of Saap Body Fur, Z-Lon, or similar material.

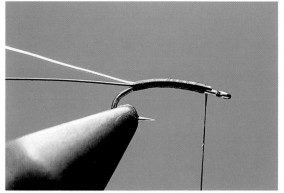

Step 1. Tie in two strands of wire behind the hook eye. Wrap thread over the wire to the hook bend to form a smooth underbody.

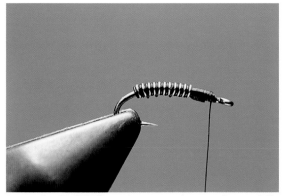

Step 2. Hold the wires together and carefully wrap them up the shank. Don't let the wires cross; you want a smooth body with alternate bands of color.

Step 4. Tie on the peacock herl. Make two wraps behind the wing, and finish with several wraps in front of the wing. Trim the wing to length.

Brassie variations are unlimited. Note the pronounced segmentation effect on the abdomens of the two-wire Brassies (left and center).

There are unlimited variations of the two-strand Brassie. You can use small metal, clear, or colored-glass beads for the heads, or different gauges of wire to create flies with different sink rates.

Murphy also modified and downsized a wire-bodied fly created by the well-known Colorado fly tier John Barr. Barr's Beadhead Copper John seems like the ideal cross between the original Pheasant Tail and the Brassie. Murphy's rendition has tails made of pheasant-tail fibers, a copper or red wire abdomen, a peacock-herl thorax with a Flashabou or Krystal Flash wing case, dyed mallard or lemon wood-duck legs, and a silver or gold beadhead. Once again, there is wide latitude for variations.

A TINY COPPER JOHN

Hook:	TMC 100, sizes 18 to 20.
Thread:	Black 8/0 to 14/0.
Tail:	Pheasant-tail fibers.
Abdomen:	Copper wire.
Wing case:	Pearlescent Mylar or a similar synthetic.
Thorax:	Peacock herl.
Legs (optional):	Dyed mallard or lemon wood duck.
Beadhead:	Gold, silver, or your choice.
Note:	This is Rick Murphy's variation of a pattern created by John Barr. Feel free to experiment with different colors.

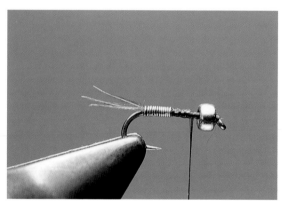

Step 2. Trim the ends of the wire and crimp them close to the hook shank. A drop of lacquer or Super Glue can be spread over the wire to further secure it, but it's not necessary.

of the hook shank. You eliminate bulk and create a smooth body by not tying the wire to the hook shank.

Step 1. Slip the bead onto the hook. Tie on the tail. Wind a smooth layer of thread over the hook shank. Take a strand of copper wire and, starting at the tail, tightly wind it around half the length

Step 3. Tie on Mylar and peacock herl.

Step 4. Wind the peacock herl forward to create the thorax. Pull the Mylar wing case over the thorax and tie it off.

Step 5. Trim the excess Mylar. The thread can be whip-finished behind the bead at this point to complete the fly, or legs may be added (see steps 6 and 7).

Step 6. Tie on dyed mallard or lemon wood-duck legs on either side of the hook shank.

Step 7. Whip-finish the thread behind the bead to finish the fly.

One of the most compelling aspects of wire flies is that they can be fished using standard dead-drift nymphing tactics and strike indicators, or cast to dimpling trout without additional weight on the leader or a strike indicator. The weight of the wire forces the fly through the surface film and into the strike zone one or two inches below the surface. I am particularly fond of using wire flies when sight-fishing to trout working clear, shallow water. It's a great way to fish a small nymph and is actually more in line with the nymph-fishing techniques Skues and Sawyer developed on the British chalk streams.

The kicker is that these flies are easy to tie and durable. And because coated wire doesn't oxidize, you can tie as many as you'll need in advance. It's as good a case for getting wired as I can come up with.

CHAPTER SIX

Getting Down— Weight for Small Flies

It doesn't take a lot of research to understand the necessity of adding weight to small flies. A few hours with a fly rod will tell you that the trout tend to lock in on midge larvae near the streambed. They also attack emerging midge pupae throughout the water column as they ascend to the surface. Consistent angling success lies in getting an imitation of the natural to the subsurface level where the trout are looking for it. This means using flies that sink. For the small-fly enthusiast, that's not always as easy as it sounds.

The development of the Brassie on Colorado's South Platte River in the 1960s alerted tiers to the possibilities of using small-gauge copper wire to add flash, segmentation, and weight to small flies. The drawback of the Brassie was that tiers were pretty much stuck with a copper body, though the better scroungers came up with red and green wire from discarded electric-motor armatures. Some small-gauge gold and silver wire was also available, but with the exception of the occasional gold-wire Brassie it was seldom used.

Extending the color range of small flies by dubbing over the Brassie's copper-wire body was attempted, but this created too much bulk. Some careful tiers were able to make properly propor-

tioned flies on hook sizes 20 through 24 by making one to three wraps of .010-inch lead wire in the thorax area. Tiny Brassies or flies weighted with lead wire under the thoraxes are ideal for fishing to trout eating midges in backwaters or in the slow water up against a bank. These situations require just enough weight to help a size 20 to 24 pupa or emerger imitation break through the surface tension when tied to a 6X or 7X tippet.

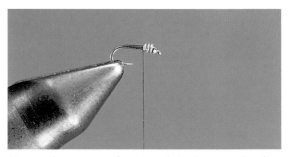

One to three wraps of .010-inch lead wire under the thorax of a size 24 hook will add weight without too much bulk.

Small-fly enthusiasts were diligently working on other alternatives when the dead-drift nymphing craze swept through the Rocky Mountains. "Dead drifters" simply attached enough weight to their leaders to get the flies down. This highly effective dead-drift nymphing technique allowed tiers to concentrate on pattern design, without worrying about how to get the flies to sink.

Interest in weighting small flies returned with the introduction of brass beads from Europe. The first beads were too large for flies smaller than size 16 or 18. The introduction of 2-millimeter beads solved this problem and tiers could begin to weight flies as small as size 26. Most fly fishers incorporated the tiny beadhead flies into their dead-drift nymphing rigs. The beadhead is flashy, and it fishes closer to the streambed than an unweighted fly fished with weight on the leader. Today, 2-millimeter beads are available in an increasing variety of colors and heavy tungsten versions.

NEW WEIGHTING IDEAS

Small-fly specialists are now seeing more options for weighting small flies. Wapsi Fly's Ultra Wire is the newest idea for adding weight to small flies. The copper-core wire comes in four sizes, two of which are important for tying small flies. The 34 gauge (.0075 inch) is suitable for size 26 or possibly size 28 hooks. The 32-gauge "Brassie wire" (.0095 inch) works on hook sizes 18 through 22.

Ultra Wires come in twenty-four colors, including traditional "shiny" as well as flat "bug" colors and hot fluorescents. The bug colors are especially interesting. The olive (two shades), gray, and brown look particularly good.

The wire can be produced in this array of colors because copper wire is now produced with a polyurethane and nylon overcoating. The clear version of this coating is what has kept your copper Brassie wire from oxidizing for the past ten or fifteen years. It was only a matter of time before a variety of colors became available in the poly-nylon coatings. Needless to say, the possibilities for very small wire-bodied flies have increased tremendously.

Another recent development is the introduction of Quick Descent Dub by Hareline Dubbin.

Wapsi Fly's Ultra Wire comes in 24 colors. The small Ultra Wire is 34 gauge (.0075-inch diameter); the next size up, Brassie wire, is 32 gauge (.0095-inch diameter). Use these wires to weight flies tied on hook sizes 18 to 26. Note that some of the colors such as the olive come in a flat "buggy" color rather than the more typical shiny hue.

Hareline Dubbin's Quick Descent Dub is made of fine strands of aluminum. Quick Descent Dub comes in 14 colors and can be dubbed very fine.

Quick Descent Dub is a fine, flashy, aluminum-based dubbing. The amazing thing about this material is that it can be finely dubbed on tying thread for use on small flies. Quick Descent Dub comes in fourteen colors.

REAL-WORLD TESTS

I tested the ability of the various materials I've mentioned to adequately weight small flies. For

Hareline Dubbin's Quick Descent Dub is easy to apply to the thread in the very small portions required when tying small flies. Pictured here is a size 24 hook.

Quick Descent Dub dubs nicely proportioned fly bodies even on this size 24 hook.

one test, I poured water into a long, clear casserole dish that was about three inches deep. I decided to tie a number of flies using various combinations of weighting materials to see if they could break the water's surface tension, and to determine how quickly they would sink. I tied flies on size 24 Tiemco TMC 100 hooks. Each fly in the test was tied to a piece of 6X tippet material with a four-wrap clinch knot. I held each fly and tippet five inches above and parallel to the water and dropped it to the surface.

Needless to say, on-stream conditions are considerably more varied. My test simulated a very soft, delicate presentation in which the fly and leader float gently to the surface, but a riffled surface and a harder landing would probably allow the fly to sink more easily. I figured that if a fly broke the surface tension under my test conditions, it would probably do the same when actually fishing.

I also decided to test the imitations while they were dry. Though a fly usually remains wet with just one false cast, and thus sinks more readily, I believe that a size 24 fly dries quickly with just one or two false casts. It was crucial that the flies

The two control flies for the test were (left to right) a dubbed (Superfine) body and thorax (Test Fly 1) and a Micro Tubing body with a thread head (Test Fly 2).

be tied to tippets for this test. A quick trial had proved that almost any size 24 nymph, larva, or pupa imitation not attached to a tippet will immediately sink. This was the first surprise—it's really the tippet that keeps small flies from sinking.

For the purpose of these tests I tied eight flies with various combinations of weighting materials and two "control" flies. I tied one control fly with an abdomen and thorax of Umpqua Superfine synthetic dubbing, the other with an abdomen of

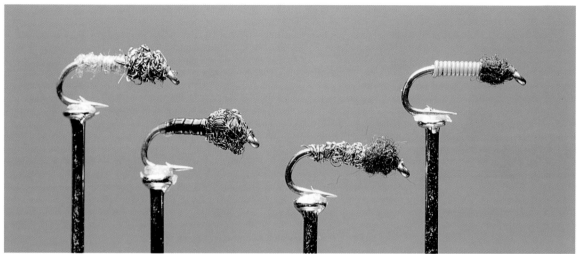

The first four weighted test flies were (left to right) body dubbed with Superfine, thorax dubbed with Quick Descent (Test Fly 3); Micro Tubing body, thorax dubbed with Quick Descent (Test Fly 4); Quick Descent body, thorax dubbed with Superfine (Test Fly 5); and wire body, thorax dubbed with Superfine (Test Fly 6).

The final four weighted test flies were (left to right) wire body, thorax dubbed with Quick Descent (Test Fly 7); body dubbed with Superfine, 2 turns .010-inch lead wire under a thorax dubbed with Superfine (Test Fly 8); body dubbed with Superfine, 2mm Spirit River bead (Test Fly 9); and wire body, 2mm Spirit River bead (Test Fly 10).

Hareline Micro Tubing and a thread head. All the flies in the test were tied with 10/0 Gudebrod thread. Below are the flies and the test results.

Most of the test results were what I expected. The flies tied with combinations of 2-millimeter beads, Ultra Wires, and wraps of .010-inch lead wire covered with Superfine dubbing sank the quickest. The biggest surprise was that the flies dubbed with the Quick Descent Dub had difficulty breaking the surface tension. The fly that had an abdomen made of Superfine dubbing and a thorax of Quick Descent Dub actually floated higher than a fly made entirely out of Superfine dubbing.

I tied another fly with an abdomen of Quick Descent Dub and a thorax of Superfine dubbing, and it didn't break the surface tension unless I jiggled the container a little. A possible explana-tion for this could be that Quick Descent Dub possesses the mass to help sink a larger fly on which more of it is used, but when a small amount is used on a tiny fly the surface area of the dubbing on the water overcomes the rela-tively light mass of the aluminum dubbing, and the fly floats.

It should also be noted that the type of mate-rial used to make small flies will affect their abil-ity to sink in calm water. Superfine dubbing will float a size 24 hook, but Micro Tubing will sink it. A body dubbed with rabbit underfur might very well sink if the fur is wet, but float if it is dry.

FISHING WEIGHTED SMALL FLIES

One type of fishing I enjoy is stalking the quiet water along stream edges for midging "bankers."

FLY	SINK CHARACTERISTIC
1. Dubbed (Superfine) body and thorax.	Gets caught in surface film, stays on top.
2. Micro Tubing body, thread head.	Sinks at a moderate rate upon hitting surface.
3. Body dubbed with Superfine; thorax dubbed with Quick Descent.	Gets caught in surface film, rides high on the surface.
4. Micro Tubing body, thorax of Quick Descent.	Gets caught in surface film, rides high on the surface.
5. Quick Descent body, thorax dubbed with Superfine.	Floats in surface film on contact.
6. Wire body, thorax dubbed with Superfine.	Sinks moderately fast on contact.
7. Wire body, thorax dubbed with Quick Descent.	Sinks moderately fast on contact (same as number 6).
8. Body dubbed with Superfine, two turns .010 fuse wire under thorax dubbed with Superfine.	Rapid descent on contact, often captures small bubble of air.
9. Body dubbed with Superfine, 2mm Spirit River bead.	Same as number 8.
10. Wire body, 2mm Spirit River bead.	Very rapid descent.

It's amazing how often large trout are overlooked so close to the bank. A small, weighted fly is perfect for this fishing. It has enough mass to break through the surface and drift to a trout feeding in one of these tight-to-the-bank spots. By using various combinations of wire, beads, and Quick Descent Dub, it's possible to develop flies with somewhat different sink rates or even neutral buoyancy.

But from a tactical standpoint in this situation, a weighted fly is all you need. You can take the strike indicator and weight off the leader. It takes a little practice to develop the skills to fish such a fly, but it's really as simple as getting in close without spooking the trout (approach from straight downstream along the bank), making your presentation, and watching the trout. You'll see it take the fly. There's nothing more exciting,

and it's as close as you'll ever get to the way G. E. M. Skues fished his nymph imitations 100 years ago.

There are a variety of materials available nowadays with which to tie weighted small flies that will sink. Some of these materials give you the ability to put a fast-sinking fly (perhaps tied with a 2-millimeter bead and dubbing, or a bead and wire) in front of a trout one to three feet below a calm surface. Furthermore, you can tie moderately weighted flies using combinations of beads, wire, and dubbing to create slow-sinking imitations to fish at the exact level where the trout are looking for food.

I'm jazzed about all these possibilities for weighting small flies. The materials give me many options to stalk trout on my own terms without adding weight or a strike indicator to the leader.

CHAPTER SEVEN

Midge Larvae and Midge Pupae

My friend Gary Willmart fishes the upper section of the San Juan River's trophy-trout water in northwestern New Mexico as well as anyone I know. He's been a guide there for decades and has seen a lot of days on the river between the renowned Texas Hole and Navajo Dam.

Gary will tell you that the most important food source for the trout are midges. It makes sense once you understand that Navajo Dam is a classic bottom-release tailwater. Water temperatures stay in the 40s throughout the year on the upper section of the river. The cold water temperatures restrict the kinds of aquatic insects that can survive in the river. Of course, the infamous San Juan worm, an aquatic annelid, is present, but in terms of sheer numbers, density, and biomass, the tiny midges of the order Diptera rule.

Both San Juan worms and the midges live in the upper San Juan for the same reason. The silty bottomed, organically rich backwaters, sloughs, and channels provide the perfect habitat, especially for members of the huge family of midges known as Chironomidae. Put another way, midges and midge imitations are your bread and butter if you guide on the upper San Juan.

I've always respected guide-style fly tying. It's a no-frills approach based on easy-to-tie, durable patterns that catch fish. The very best guide flies have an undeniable elegance, too. Al Troth's unbeatable Elk Hair Caddis is in this group. Other guide-style flies are simple "meat and potatoes" dressings that catch fish after fish. Most guides will tell you that 80 to 90 percent of their client hookups are made on these simple, rugged flies. More fragile or difficult-to-tie flies may be held in reserve, just in case a guide has to pull a trip out of the fire, but are seldom seen on a day-to-day basis.

Years ago Gary showed me his amazingly simple but highly effective method for imitating the tremendous variety of midge larvae (sometimes erroneously called worms or annelids because they look like tiny worms) that he encounters in the San Juan River. Gary actually does what all the writers back to Ernest Schwiebert in *Matching the Hatch* implore anglers to do. When necessary, he carefully pumps a stomach sample from a trout and matches what he sees. Usually that amounts to a gut full of midge larvae in several sizes and colors. He imitates the most numerous midges in the sample,

How important are midge larvae? Here's what a San Juan River trout had in its stomach. The Thread Midge Larva in the lower center of the photograph is a good match.

paying particular attention to size, segmentation, overall color, and color of the head.

The next part of Gary's approach is what spooks the "pretty boy" fly tiers. He sits down at the tying vise and makes a simple imitation completely out of 8/0 thread, matching the base color of the body with one thread and then ribbing it with the right color of thread to bring out the subtleties of the natural's segmentation. Gary finishes the fly with an oversized thread head (usually black) to match the natural. His choice of hook is the curved, fine-wire Tiemco TMC 2487 because it closely approximates what a midge larva looks like when swept into the water column. If he wants a little "longer" imitation, he goes to the Tiemco TMC 200R.

Most midge larva patterns are similarly shaped, but materials can be varied to enhance brightness, translucency, or segmentation. Pictured left to right: Chocolate Midge Larva (dubbed synthetic), Brassie (wire), Thread Midge Larva (thread), Biot Larva (goose biot), and Miracle Nymph (floss over black thread base).

THREAD MIDGE LARVA

Hook:	TMC 2487, TMC 200R, Daiichi 1130, Daiichi 1140, sizes 18 to 24.
Thread:	8/0 to 14/0.
Abdomen:	8/0 to 14/0 thread to match natural.
Rib:	8/0 to 14/0 thread to imitate segmentation of natural.

Head:	Black thread, tied oversized.
Note:	Amazingly accurate imitations of midges can be made with only thread. Wind the thread evenly over the hook shank to produce a thin body with no "lumps."

The Thread Midge Larva.

"I wish I could make it harder, but this just *works* the best," Gary says.

I've had a few quiet little talks with my professional fly-tying pals about guide-style fly tying and they all agree that the simple meat-and-potatoes flies do catch fish. "It's just that they don't catch fishermen," they say. To a person, they requested that I not quote them by name.

If you're a fly-tying junkie, you'll find that midge larvae will provide relatively slim pickings. But if you're like me, you will still find ways to complicate things. For a while I was dyeing *thread* to get the colors I wanted. Other intricacies include considering what the thread will look like when wet and getting the segmentation just right. Most of the midge fishermen I run with agree that correctly imitating the subtle light and dark variations created by the larva's segmentation can make a difference in pattern effectiveness.

MATERIALS FOR TYING LARVA AND PUPA IMITATIONS

There is also the matter of materials. Although all midge larva imitations tend to have a wormlike shape, different materials create different effects. Tightly dubbed natural materials such as beaver or muskrat are another way to represent midge larva segmentation. Stripped-quill abdomens have a different look than do those made of thread. Mallard, teal, or gadwall barbs wound around a hook shank can make excellent midge larva imitations. A goose biot wrapped around a hook with either the rough side up or the smooth side up creates superb segmentation. The use of peacock or ostrich as a thorax or head is a more lively alternative to simply winding an enlarged thread head.

The use of synthetics extends the possibilities even further. Ultra-fine synthetic dubbings, which are available in a mind-boggling range of colors, can be tightly dubbed to create excellent segmentation. Flashier blends that include Antron-like materials are also available in an equally large array of colors.

DISCO MIDGE

Hook:	TMC 200R, TMC 2487, sizes 18 to 24.	Abdomen:	Krystal Flash or Accent Flash. Red, pearlescent, blue (in winter), and olive are popular colors.
Thread:	8/0 to 14/0.		
Abdomen underbody:	Thread bases of different colors will change the effect.	Thorax/head:	Peacock herl, hare's-ear dubbing, or oversized black thread.

The Disco Midge.

The well-known Disco Midge series, originated on Colorado's Frying Pan River, uses a flashy synthetic, such as Krystal Flash, wrapped around the hook shank as an abdomen. The head is peacock. Krystal Flash comes in a lot of colors, but red still tops the list because it imitates numerous chironomid species common to trout waters. Pearlescent Krystal Flash tied over a white thread underbody is a flashy alternative to red.

MIRACLE NYMPH

Hook:	TMC 100, TMC 101, or similar hook, sizes 18 to 24.
Abdomen underbody:	Black thread, 8/0 to 14/0.
Abdomen overbody:	White floss.
Rib:	Fine copper wire.
Thorax/head:	Black 8/0 to 14/0 thread.
Note:	Vary the thread underbody color to obtain different shades, but keep the oversized thorax and head black. Be sure to wrap the underbody evenly.

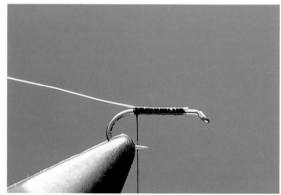

Step 2. Tie in a piece of fine copper wire. Wrap an even layer of black thread over it toward the hook eye and then wrap an even layer back toward the hook bend.

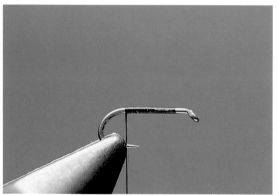

Step 1. Wrap a single, even layer of black thread toward the rear of the hook.

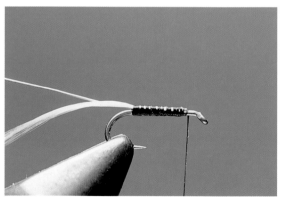

Step 3. Tie in the white floss. Wrap the thread toward the hook eye, forming an even underbody of thread.

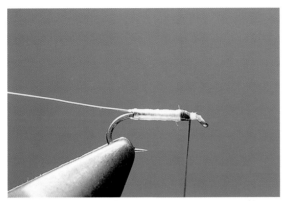

Step 4. Wind the floss forward and tie it off.

Step 5. Rib the abdomen with the copper wire and tie it off.

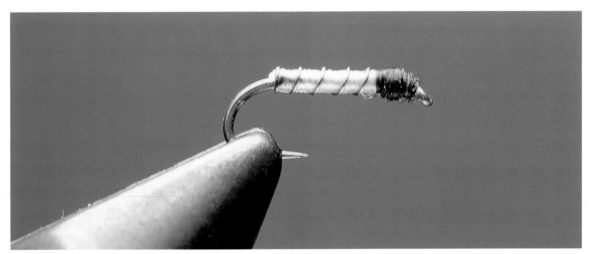

Step 6. Form an oversize black head.

Translucence can be especially important when making up midge larva imitations. The Miracle Nymph, a famous South Platte River midge imitation, relies heavily on this property. The fly is tied with a black thread underbody topped with white floss and ribbed with fine copper wire. The head is black thread. When the fly is wet it has a shimmery gray tone that is deadly on midging trout, especially when they are working deep. I tie Miracle Nymphs with several different color threads as underbodies for different effects. I've found a yellow underbody with a black head to be especially effective at times. You should also consider the impact of different colored thread underbodies when using synthetics in the Disco Midge series.

THE MERCURY MIDGE

The Mercury Midge is an improved version of the Miracle Nymph. The beauty of the Miracle Nymph to me has always been its simplicity. Pat Dorsey, a longtime South Platte River guide (and no relation to an inventive fly tier of the same name based in Miami), is the originator of the

Mercury Midge. Pat improved the Miracle Nymph by tying it on a curved-shank Tiemco TMC 2487 hook and adding a tiny, silver-lined clear bead.

"Bill Black at Spirit River sent me these micro beads," says Dorsey. "I then took the cream thread and copper rib—thinking about how really effective the Miracle Nymph has always been for me on the South Platte River—and added the little bead. The first thing that struck me was how it looked like mercury from a thermometer because it's a silver-lined bead. So that's how the name Mercury Midge came about."

Pat said that he experimented with the pattern on the South Platte and was surprised to see trout moving an unheard-of ten to twelve inches from their feeding lies to take the fly.

"I thought, 'Holy Cow, this thing is incredible!' I knew it was something about the bead. What was weird was how all of a sudden everyone was talking about the Mercury Midge. I'd pull up a fishing report from the Arkansas River and they were talking about the Mercury Midge. It really was kind of cool and I'm glad the word got out. It's a good fly and I want everyone to know about it," he said.

DORSEY'S MERCURY MIDGE

Hook: Dai-Riki 135 or TMC 2487, sizes 18 to 24.
Thread: White Flymaster 6/0.
Head: Spirit River Hi-Lite silver glass bead, extra small.

Body: White Flymaster 6/0.
Rib: Fine copper wire, reverse wrapped.

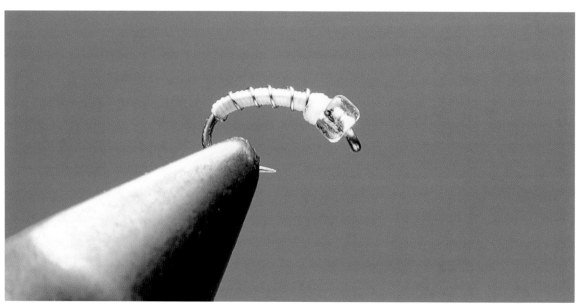

The Mercury Midge.

Dorsey ties the Mercury Midge on a Tiemco TMC 2487 hook in sizes 18 through 24. He uses white Flymaster 6/0 thread because he likes its "kind of waxy translucence," and uses the finest copper wire he can find. Spirit River's extra-small Hi-Lite silver-lined glass bead adds the all-important flash to the fly.

Since coming up with the Mercury Midge, Dorsey has taken other standard South Platte River flies and modified them to include the Hi-Lite glass beads. He ties a Mercury Pheasant-Tail Nymph, Mercury RS-2, Mercury Brassie, Mercury *Baetis* Nymph, Mercury PMD, and Mercury Blood Midge.

THE BLACK BEAUTY

Dorsey is also responsible for another Rocky Mountain midge pattern: the Black Beauty. The Black Beauty has saved the day for many a fly fisher on difficult western tailwaters and spring creeks.

"I came up with the Black Beauty one day after I'd seen so many midge shucks along the edge of the river that I could literally sweep my finger across the surface of the water and pick them up like icing off a cake. That's when I realized how critical midge pupae are to a trout's diet. From there it was fairly simple. I just tried to come up with a black midge pupa imitation. It's such a silly, simple pattern. There's an 8/0 black Uni-thread body, a fine copper-wire rib, and a bulbous head of black synthetic dubbing," Dorsey told me.

I should say that it has been my experience over many years of fishing "technical" small-fly tailwaters and spring creeks that the "silly, simple patterns" are often the most productive. Dorsey's Black Beauty is no exception. It's a must-have pattern on the South Platte River.

There are a number of useful variations of the Black Beauty. The Black Beauty Emerger adds a bit of white Z-Lon just behind the thorax. Another variation incorporates a black micro bead and, needless to say, another variation utilizes the Spirit River Hi-Lite silver glass bead.

Dorsey's patterns prove that the silver-lined bead is here to stay on Rocky Mountain tailwaters and spring creeks, and it could very well

The Black Beauty, designed by South Platte River guide Pat Dorsey, has become a standard midge pattern throughout the Rocky Mountains. It's a simple fly (black thread body, copper rib, fine black synthetic dubbing for thorax) that can be tied in many interesting, fish-catching variations.

improve your favorite local patterns. More than anything, the silver beads add just another piece to the puzzle for fly fishers interested in catching trout with small flies in difficult waters.

The Brassie, Gene Lynch's well-known South Platte River midge larva imitation, uses fine cop-per wire to form a nicely segmented and flashy abdomen. Wire now available in a variety of colors creates additional options. Some tiers simply make the Brassie's head out of thread (black or red), while others prefer a fuller peacock collar.

LARVA LACE DEEP MIDGE PUPA

Hook:	TMC 200R, sizes 16 to 20.
Thread:	Olive 8/0 to 14/0.
Abdomen underbody:	Olive 8/0 to 14/0 thread or a color to match the natural.
Abdomen overbody:	Clear Larva Lace tubing.
Thorax and head:	Black rabbit underfur.
Note:	You can add two strands of pearlescent Krystal Flash at the head to further brighten the fly. Vary the color of the thread underbody to match the naturals in your area; a Krystal Flash underbody adds brightness to the fly.

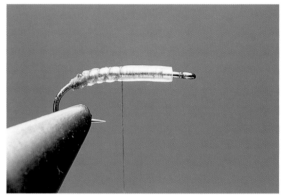

Step 2. Slide the Larva Lace all the way to the rear of the hook and tie it down. Rib the Larva Lace with the thread.

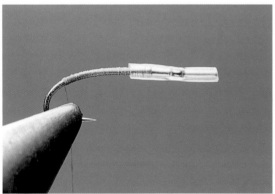

Step 1. Wrap an even layer of tying thread back to the hook bend. Slide a section of Larva Lace tubing over the hook eye.

Step 3. Dub a dark thorax and head.

Step 4. Add two strands of Krystal Flash at the head.

Step 5. Trim the Krystal Flash to length and whip-finish the head.

Tubelike or solid synthetics such as Larva Lace, pioneered by Phil Camera, are important for larva imitations. These materials may be stretched and wrapped around the hook shank or, in the case of the tubelike stuff, slipped over the hook shank and ribbed with thread. The material is soft and creates realistic segmentation. Tubing is available in a variety of colors that can be further enhanced by using different colored threads or flashy synthetics as underbodies.

Midge larva imitations are typically dead-drifted near the bottom in rivers or allowed to well up in the water column to imitate larvae that have been dislodged into the drift. When you observe the bulging riseforms so typical of midging trout, you can be sure that the fish are eating pupae rather than midge larvae.

Fishing tactics for midge larva and pupa imitations revolve around the idea that any midge larvae in the water column have gotten there by mistake, whereas pupae in the water column typically signal the beginning of a midge hatch. Most midge fishers agree that the majority of trout landed on midge imitations are taken with pupa imitations. Pupa patterns can be fished using dead-drift nymphing techniques, particularly at the beginning of the hatch. Fishing pupa imitations becomes considerably more exciting as the hatch progresses toward the surface, where the trout feed on them, creating bulging riseforms.

Midge fishers also agree that trout feeding on midge pupae demand special patterns. Most often these imitations are simply variations of larva designs that incorporate the pupa's increased swimming activity, a larger thorax and head area with the clear indication of wing pads, and different coloration.

ADDING FLASH

Among the most important characteristics of the ascending midge pupa are the gases that it uses to fill the pupal skin to aid its rise to the surface. J. R. Harris in his groundbreaking *An Angler's Entomology,* published in 1956, describes the gases as being so reflective at some angles as to make the color of an emerging nymph hard to determine. He later describes an emerging chironomid pupa that "assumes a much increased lustre, and in fact strongly resembles a section of a glass tube which has been filled with mercury."

From an angling and fly-tying point of view, I divide midge pupae into two groups. I use the term "deep pupa" or just "midge pupa" to describe the relatively simple patterns I use to imitate the pupa as it ascends through the water column to the surface. "Midge emerger" describes

Midge pupa imitations for deep fishing should reflect light or suggest swimming pupae. The Disco Midge (left) is a flashy fly. The Chocolate Midge Pupa (center) with a few strands of Krystal Flash is more subdued. The Micro Soft-Hackle (right) suggests a swimming pupa.

the pupa once it has reached the surface, where it either hangs vertically in the surface film or is positioned horizontally on the surface as the pupal shuck actually splits open. There are a number of innovative fly designs that imitate the emerger phase.

I try to incorporate the flash of the gases beneath the skin of the midge pupa in all my imitations. Sometimes overkill *will* work—and when it does, it pays to have a few pearlescent Disco Midges on hand. Their bright abdomens are as close to Harris's "glass tube of mercury" as you can get, and the peacock thoraxes are good representations of the enlarged thoraxes and heads of many emerging naturals.

More often than not, though, I've found that understating the flash makes for a more effective fly. I like an abdomen that is thinly dubbed with a fine synthetic to match the natural and ribbed with fine silver or copper wire. I dub an oversize

thorax to match the typically darker thorax, wing pads, and head. When I tie off the head, I lay a few short pieces of pearlescent Krystal Flash at an angle up over the top of the thorax—just enough to get the trout's attention. If I want a little more flash in the fly, I use a flashier fine synthetic dubbing for the abdomen.

THE MICRO SOFT-HACKLE

Another option is the Micro Soft-Hackle, a guide fly I came up with twenty years ago. Tying it is as simple as dubbing a thin body of dyed rabbit underfur to match the natural and then winding a soft hackle with the downlike aftershaft feather found at the base of a partridge body feather. The stem of the aftershaft is very thin, and it takes some practice to learn to make a wind or two without breaking it. Once you've wound the hackle, simply stroke it back and make a few wraps of thread over it so it flares to the rear.

Adding a few short strands of Krystal Flash at the head of a Chocolate Midge Larva (left) may be enough to make it effective as an emerging midge pupa (right).

ENGLE'S MICRO SOFT-HACKLE FLY

Hook: TMC 100, TMC 101, or similar hook, sizes 18 to 22.

Thread: Black 8/0 to 14/0.

Abdomen: Olive rabbit underfur or a color to match the midges in your area.

Rib: Fine gold wire.

Hackle: Partridge aftershaft feather.

Note: Select smaller aftershaft plumes for smaller flies. Winding the fluffy hackle requires a very light touch. You can brighten up the pattern with a fine gold rib or a few strands of Krystal Flash tied in at the head.

Step 2. Dub a thin body of rabbit underfur.

Here's a partridge feather with the downlike aftershaft plume still attached.

Step 3. Tie in the partridge aftershaft feather.

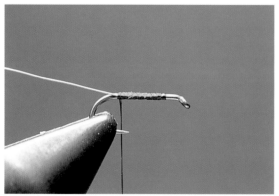

Step 1. Tie on the gold wire rib.

Step 4. Carefully wrap the feather around the hook shank two or three times.

Step 5. Stroke the hackle back toward the rear of the hook.

The advantage of the Micro Soft-Hackle is that it readily absorbs water. The aftershaft feather has great action in the water that imitates the swimming midge pupa. If you want to add a little flash to the imitation, just tie in a short piece of Krystal Flash at the head, or rib the abdomen with fine silver wire. This pattern, along with the previous deep-water pupa, can be cast to bulging trout or dead-drifted deep when you first spot the trout flashing in the current as they pick off pupae emerging from the streambed. When the trout are feeding near the bottom, it also pays to try a Brassie, Miracle Nymph, or Disco Midge. Fish these patterns to tailing trout that are grabbing midge pupae right when they come out of the streambed silt.

Don't hesitate to test any variations of the standard patterns that you may dream up. These are easy flies to tie, and sometimes the smallest variation will turn out to be the trigger you need to fool difficult trout.

Step 6. Complete the fly with an oversize black head.

CHAPTER EIGHT

Midges on Top and in the Surface Film

The saving grace of the long winters where I live in Colorado is the knowledge that in February there will be a midge hatch of some magnitude on the South Platte River. For those of us who find life depressing without the rises of trout, the February midge hatch brings hope. It is those midging trout that pull us through to the blue-winged olives in April.

Midging trout make the most beautiful rise-forms. I've witnessed gorgeous full head-to-tail porpoising rises on warm February mornings and, on the best days, startling backwater rises where the trout appear to rise very slowly and almost vertically out of the water to take the midges and then slide back down along the exact same path.

Many midging riseforms, or smutting rises as the British refer to them (after a black fly known as a reed smut), seem to indicate that trout are taking food that may be in a compromised position. The fish aren't slashing the water's surface. They aren't quick-turning downstream to chase after a rapidly emerging bug. They are simply and methodically feeding on a food source that seems to be helpless.

A closer examination of a hatch of midges reveals that this casual feeding attitude is due to the fact that the trout are taking crippled midges, or more likely midges that are in the process of emerging from their pupal shucks. Once out of their shucks, midges are quickly airborne.

IMITATING TRAILING SHUCKS

Even closer examination of a hatch of midges on the water's surface reveals large numbers of insects stuck in their pupal shucks. You can learn something if you closely examine this shuck. First, you'll see that the midge, which is a member of that huge order of two-winged flies known as Diptera, has a hard shuck. You'll see whole shucks floating on the water's surface or piled high in scum lines near the bank. The sections of the abdomen and the thorax are clearly visible. Compared to a typical mayfly shuck, the midge shuck retains considerably more structural integrity when it is shed.

It also pays to note the color of the shuck. Most midges have gray to olive-gray shucks, but I have also observed some that ranged from amber to dirty yellow. I have found that matching the color of a midge's pupal shuck has improved the effectiveness of some of my imitations.

Once you've spent some time observing hatching midges and how the trout respond to

The material used for a trailing shuck is a factor when designing midge emergers. Pictured from left to right: ostrich feather, amber Antron, white Antron, grizzly hackle barbs, wood-duck flank, and muskrat underfur (guard hair tips removed).

those hatches, it becomes clear that almost any surface midge imitation or in-the-film midge imitation will be more effective if it has some sort of trailing shuck. Over the past few years I've reduced my adult midge imitations to a very few general patterns that include the irreplaceable Griffith's Gnat, several colors of palmer-hackled dry flies, and a smattering of fore-and-aft-hackled drys, such as that western standby the Renegade, tied size 20 and smaller.

My trailing-shuck midge patterns are another story. I think it pays to experiment with different materials when it comes to the all-important shuck. I'm fond of shiny synthetics such as Z-Lon and Antron. Natural materials such as muskrat (with the guard hairs removed), mallard flank (the natural barring imitates abdominal segments), wood-duck flank, or even a few hackle

barbs can make an effective shuck imitation. The trick is to have patterns with several different types of shucks, particularly if the trout turn picky. It may be that one particular shuck material will be the trigger that induces the trout to strike.

Besides adding a trailing shuck, you must also consider the attitude of the fly in the surface film. There are two distinct attitudes that emerging midges take. "Suspender" patterns are designed to imitate the midge suspended vertically just under the surface film. This type of fly typically utilizes a short post of closed-cell foam tied in at an angle at the hook eye. The foam is intended to float the fly in a nearly vertical position in the film. Roger Hill, a well-known Colorado fly fisher, fly tier, and author, uses deer hair to provide this flotation.

SUSPENDER-STYLE MIDGE

Hook:	TMC 100, TMC 101, or similar dry-fly hooks or curved-style hooks like the TMC 2487, TMC 200R, or similar models; sizes 18 to 24.	Rib (optional):	Fine gold or silver wire.
		Thorax (optional):	Sparse muskrat, hare's-ear, or similar dubbing.
Thread:	Black 8/0 to 14/0 or to match natural.	Foam post:	Closed-cell foam; white for better visibility or to match wing color of naturals. Or a clump of deer hair pulled over the thorax, tied down behind the eye, and clipped short.
Abdomen:	Thread, goose biot, pheasant tail, or dubbing to match natural.		

Suspender-style midge.

Most suspender-style midges are quite simple to tie. They imitate little more than the abdomen with or without ribbing, and sometimes a hint of the thorax and the suspending strip of foam. I've always wondered if the suspender-style midges, especially in the small sizes, really do hang vertically in the film. My tests in the field and an aquarium are inconclusive. A little tug after presentation may help them "set up," but surface tension is a strong force on a size 20 or smaller hook.

Nonetheless, these flies *do* work whether suspended vertically in the film or lying horizontally on their sides on the water's surface. A few wraps of hackle around the base of the post may help larger suspender imitations set up vertically in the film, but once again, it's hard to tell.

When I first began using suspender-style flies on the San Juan River, I assumed that the closed-cell foam was simply for flotation, and I tried to keep it as unobtrusive as possible. The meat of the pattern seemed to be the realistic representation of the midge pupa suspended vertically just on the underside of the surface film. A huge midge hatch on a small lake in northern New Mexico changed my opinion.

I was in a belly boat, where I could closely watch the hatching midges. I noted that when the adult actually began to pull its wings and body clear of the pupal shuck, it assumed a somewhat more horizontal position on the water. All you could see then was the tan color of the wings wrapped around the body emerging from the tubelike shuck. Those wings looked *exactly* like the tan closed-cell post I was using on my suspender patterns. It occurred to me that the hook might actually be representing the *shuck* of the hatching insect rather than the insect itself.

Since that time I've developed several alternative suspender patterns, each with a curved hook shank bent slightly from the horizontal and simply wound with a synthetic, such as Frostbite by Fish Hunter Enterprises, to imitate the sheen of an emptying pupal shuck. The color of the post is then simply matched to the wing color of the hatching midge. I add a sparse thorax of peacock or dubbing to match the natural. A few wraps of hackle at the base of the post help to float the fly and may represent some of the commotion of the adult clambering out of the shuck.

EMERGENT ADULT MIDGE—SUSPENDER STYLE

Hook: TMC 200R, bent slightly, sizes 18 to 20.
Thread: Gray 8/0 to 14/0.
Shuck: Olive Frostbite or similar synthetic wrapped around the shank. Frostbite is a fine, translucent, stretchy braid distributed to the trade by Hareline Dubbin. It's a little easier to work with if you put it on a bobbin.
Thorax: Peacock herl.
Foam post: Tan closed-cell foam or a color to match the wings of the natural.
Hackle: Grizzly tied parachute style at the base of the post.

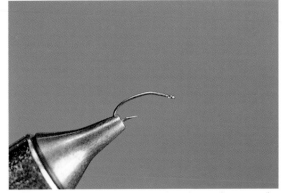

Step 1. Slightly bend the hook to form a flat platform near the eye.

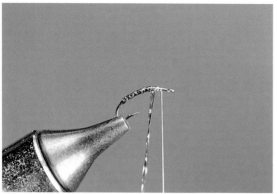

Step 2. Wrap the rear portion of the hook with Frostbite to form a trailing shuck.

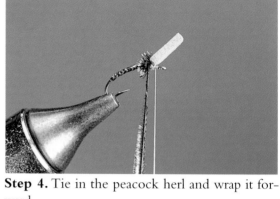

Step 4. Tie in the peacock herl and wrap it forward.

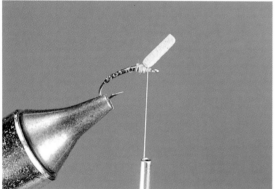

Step 3. Tie in the foam post.

Step 5. Mount the grizzly hackle at the hook eye.

Step 6. Wrap a few turns of grizzly hackle around the base of the foam post, tie off the hackle, form a head, and whip-finish.

The other major group of surface-film midge patterns includes those that lie horizontally in the film. These patterns emphasize a trailing shuck and the emerging midge adult, or a configuration where the emerging adult is stuck in the shuck.

ROGER HILL'S STILLBORN MIDGE

Hook: Partridge K1A, TMC 100, TMC 501, sizes 20 to 26.

Thread: Black 8/0 to 14/0.

Shuck: Muskrat fur (clean out guard hairs).

Thorax: Peacock herl.

Hackle: Grizzly.

Note: This is one of the most effective midge patterns I know. It and other patterns appear in Roger Hill's excellent but out-of-print book, *Fly Fishing the South Platte River.*

Use only the *underfur* to make the trailing shuck on Hill's Stillborn Midge.

Hill's Stillborn Midge.

Roger Hill's Stillborn Midge is the best trailing-shuck pattern I've found and is a good example of how simple an effective midge pattern can be. It's the materials that count. The forward portion of the fly is nothing more than the classic Griffith's Gnat with the peacock body and palmered grizzly hackle. It's the trailing shuck that makes the difference. Hill uses a wisp of muskrat from which the guard hairs have been removed. He strives to get the silvery blue underfur with brown tips. The pattern is dynamite.

STUCK-IN-THE-SHUCK MIDGE

Hook:	TMC 100, TMC 101, or similar dry-fly hook, sizes 18 to 22.
Thread:	Gray 8/0 to 14/0, or to match the natural.
Shuck:	Amber Antron or a similar synthetic.
Wing:	Loop of white Z-Lon. Foam may be substituted.
Abdomen:	The tying thread.
Thorax:	Peacock herl.
Hackle:	Grizzly.

Step 1. Tie in the Antron trailing shuck.

Step 2. Tie in the white Z-Lon.

Step 3. Wind the thread forward to form the abdomen. Tie in the hackle at the front of the abdomen.

Step 4. Tie in the peacock herl.

Step 6. Wind the hackle through the peacock-herl thorax and tie it off.

Step 5. Wrap the peacock herl forward.

Step 7. Pull the Z-Lon over the back of the fly. Tie it down with a few loose wraps, and then slip a needle under it to pull it up and form a loop. Once the loop is formed, add more, tighter wraps and then trim off the excess Z-Lon. Form a head and whip-finish to complete the fly.

Another series of in-the-film midge patterns attempts to imitate emerging adults that have become stuck in their pupal shucks. The most common representation revolves around the wings being trapped in the shuck. This is best represented with a loop of wing material over the back of the pattern. A pattern that I've found quite effective where I live utilizes a trailing shuck of amber Antron or Z-Lon, an abdomen of gray thread, and a thorax of peacock herl with a few turns of grizzly hackle through it. The "stuck" wing is represented with a loop of white Z-Lon tied in at the tail and looped over the top of the entire fly.

I believe the pattern was originally created to represent a rather large size 18 midge that emerges on the South Platte River in March. This bug has a distinctive amber shuck. Since I was first introduced to the pattern I've used it throughout the West and in the East, and found that its effectiveness is not confined to the South Platte's particular hatch. If I had to guess at what

feature of the fly gives it its widespread appeal, I'd go with the amber shuck or possibly the looped wing.

The abdomen of this stuck-in-the-shuck pattern can be modified by using different colored threads to more closely match your local midge hatches. I carry them in gray, black, and light olive. Some tiers modify the looped wing by using a strip of foam rather than Z-Lon. This provides better flotation and somewhat higher visibility, but may tend to lift the fly out of the surface film. Nonetheless, it is effective and durable.

CUL-DE-CANARD EMERGERS

Any discussion of midge emergers should include the use of cul-de-canard (CDC). My experience with this material in midge-emerger patterns has varied. I believe the key is to limit the use of CDC to the wings of the fly. CDC used to represent the shuck tends to float the fly too high on the water's surface.

CDC MIDGE EMERGER

Hook:	TMC 101, TMC 100, or similar dry-fly hook, sizes 18 to 24.
Thread:	8/0 to 14/0, color to match the natural.
Shuck:	Olive Z-Lon.
Abdomen:	Olive goose biot, or a color to match the natural.
Thorax:	Gray Olive Superfine dubbing, or a color to match the natural.
Wing:	A loop of tan CDC.
Legs (optional):	A few strands of Z-Lon at the hook eye.

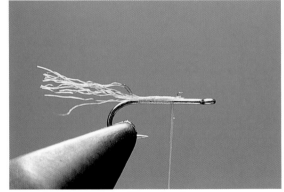

Step 1. Tie in the trailing shuck.

Step 2. Attach the goose biot.

Step 3. Wind the biot to make a smooth abdomen.

Step 4. Tie in the CDC. Tie it down loosely with the tips toward the hook eye, and then pull it through the wraps; this is easier than trying to attach the feather near the tip end.

Step 5. Dub the thorax.

Step 6. Loop the wing over the thorax. Pull the material over the thorax, make a few loose wraps of thread, and use a bodkin to pull the material up into a loop.

Step 7. Tie off and whip-finish the head.

Shane Stalcup and René Harrop have popu-larized loop-wing CDC midge and mayfly emergers. In Stalcup's version, the trailing shuck is Z-Lon tied sparse and the abdomen is a goose biot in a color to match the natural. The biot is wound smoothly, without the ridges. A loop of CDC is then made from the rear of the dubbed thorax and tied in at the eye. The CDC is tied in tips first, then the thorax is dubbed and the CDC is looped over it and tied down at the eye. The CDC gives the fly the buoyancy to stay in the surface film, but the less buoyant biot abdomen tends to settle nicely into the film.

IN-THE-FILM CDC EMERGER

Hook:	TMC 100, TMC 101, or similar dry-fly hook, sizes 18 to 24.
Thread:	Black 8/0 to 14/0 or a color to match the natural.
Shuck (optional):	Barred mallard or wood duck.
Abdomen:	The tying thread.
Thorax:	Peacock herl, tied sparse.
Wing:	Cul-de-canard tied down-wing style.

The In-the-Film CDC Emerger.

Another very simple CDC in-the-film pattern consists of a barred-mallard trailing shuck tied sparse, a thread abdomen, a sparse peacock thorax, and a short CDC wing tied in a down-wing position across the thorax. The trick is to make the CDC wing no longer than half the length of the hook shank. It's one of those fine patterns that presents well and is simple to tie. It can also be tied without the trailing shuck to represent an adult midge.

It should be clear by now that I put a lot of stock in simple and minor variations on standard themes. My experience over the years indicates that when trout get picky about emerging midges, anglers need to concentrate first on making good presentations, and second on trying to find what the trout are keying on. It might be that a more rigid, shiny trailing shuck of Z-Lon does the trick one day, whereas on another day the trout are looking for the more active, filmy

kind of trailing shuck that muskrat best represents. If you have a few patterns that cover a range of possibilities and systematically work through them, you will often hit on the right fly.

ADULT MIDGE IMITATIONS

Finally, there are a few patterns that shade a little more closely to the adult midges rather than emergers. Within this broad group I like patterns that represent drowned adults and those that depict more fully emerged wings.

Drowned-adult patterns are no more than miniature soft-hackle flies. My Micro Soft-Hackle Fly described in chapter 7 uses a soft hackle made from the aftershaft of a partridge feather. It works well as an emergent midge pupa *and* when cast as a drowned adult to rising trout.

More traditional mini soft-hackle imitations use a few wraps of standard materials such as hen or partridge. Look for smaller soft-hackle feathers

The tiny feathers found at the shoulder of a partridge or similar soft-feathered game bird make ideal soft hackles for drowned-midge wet flies.

on the leading edge of a partridge wing near the shoulder. Drowned-adult patterns may be tied with thread, quill, or biot abdomen; sparse thorax; and soft hackle. Some tiers add a short wing of Zing or similar synthetic material tied down-wing style across the top of the fly.

A drowned-midge wet fly with a thread body and a pinch of dubbing for the thorax is effective when trout are bulging to midges near the surface.

PHIL WHITE'S ADULT MIDGE

Hook:	TMC 100, TMC 101, or similar dry-fly hook, sizes 18 to 20.
Thread:	Black 8/0 to 14/0.
"Wing" or shuck:	Two strands of peacock.
Body:	Peacock herl.
Hackle:	Grizzly.

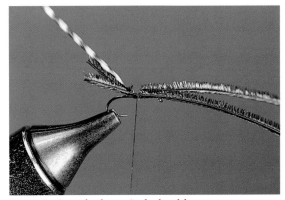

Step 3. Attach the grizzly hackle.

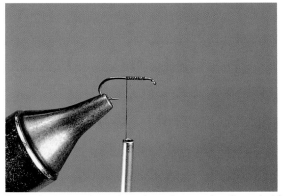

Step 1. Wrap the tying thread over the front half of the hook shank.

Step 4. Wrap the peacock herl forward to form the body.

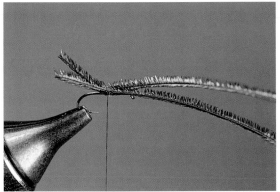

Step 2. Mount two pieces of peacock herl to form a delta "wing."

Step 5. Wrap the hackle through the herl. Tie off the hackle, form the head, and whip-finish.

Al Beatty showed me an adult midge pattern that represents one more incarnation of the Griffith's Gnat. He picked up this particular pattern from Phil White, who is the riverkeeper on the River Wye in England. The forward portion of the pattern is nothing more than a Griffith's Gnat. The rear portion is simply two "wings" of peacock herl. Whether the herl actually represents wings or a trailing shuck to the trout is immaterial. Beatty says the pattern has worked on a broad range of waters.

The bottom line is that you'll have to experiment with materials to come up with the most effective flies. Try a variety of materials for trailing shucks and test them on your local waters. Odds are you'll come up with a few favorites. The same goes for abdomen and wing materials. Subtle variations in materials may make the difference between inspection rises and the real thing. With a little luck, the gorgeous riseforms that midging trout make will be to *your* imitations.

CHAPTER NINE

Olives

The genus name *Baetis* has become popular among fly fishers to describe the numerous species of tiny mayflies characterized by slate-blue wings and olive bodies. It's a nice scientific term, but the older and more descriptive name for these mayflies, blue-winged olives, is really as technical as you need to get, and it covers a genus or two of similar mayflies *not* included in *Baetis*. Whatever you choose to call these insects, fly fishers across the United States look forward to the prolific "olives" as the first major mayfly hatch of the spring and the last good hatch in autumn.

Since there is a fair amount of variation among the different mayfly species lumped into the blue-winged olive category, it always pays to examine hatching duns. The usual and correct strategy is to try to match an imitation as closely as possible to the size, color, and silhouette of the natural, but carrying imitations to match every *Baetis* color variation is impractical. Some particularly difficult fish may require an exact color imitation, but a general-purpose dun with an abdomen of medium-brownish-olive dubbing or a dyed-olive quill will often serve admirably, especially when skillfully presented.

The nymphs of *Baetis* and associated blue-winged olive genera (*Accentrella, Procloeon, Diphetor,* and *Plauditus*) all tend to be streamlined in appearance and are noted for their swimming ability. Along with matching size and color, a paramount consideration when tying *Baetis* nymphs is to keep the silhouette sparse and thin. Once again, various shades of brown, olive, and gray are good colors.

Hatching blue-winged olives are often trapped in the surface film by turbulence or wind. Spent-wing spinner patterns are good imitations of these trapped duns.

Spent-spinner imitations can be important when fishing the blue-winged olive hatches. Where I live in the West, this is particularly true during the autumn hatches, where great spinner falls often occur just before dark. It's also important to note that spent-spinner imitations may be useful during the hatch. The dun's small size makes it susceptible to being blown over or upset by turbulent water. It's not uncommon to see large rafts of duns with their wings trapped in the surface film during a hatch. A standard poly-wing spinner works well in this situation and may save the day if the trout are unenthusiastic about your dun imitations.

It may seem like the blue-winged olive hatch is a fairly straightforward affair that can be solved with modern small-fly designs. And that is often the case for the last half of the hatch, but it's the front end of the blue-winged olive hatch that can leave fly fishers scratching their heads.

A maddening scenario often presents itself at the beginning of the hatch when the trout start chasing the emerging nymphs. *Baetis* are good swimmers, and you'll often see the fish flashing as they cut side to side chasing down the actively swimming nymphs. As the hatch progresses, the trout will station themselves along the most pro-ductive lines of drift, where they snatch the emerging nymphs now making their way closer and closer to the surface. The trout's feeding is often revealed by bulges, head-to-tail porpoising riseforms, boils, and the lumbering head-to-tail rise that ends with a satisfied wiggle of the tail. Ray Bergman called it the "satisfaction rise." Anglers who have fished over trout performing the satisfaction rise will testify that they are some of the most difficult risers to catch. In his book *Small Fly Adventures in the West: A Guide to Angling for Larger Trout,* Neal Streeks puts it nicely: "The prospects seem so good and alluring, but the trout's narrow-mindedness can be exasperating. . . ."

RS-2

It's the front end of the blue-winged olive hatch that keeps me coming back to the water and the fly-tying vise. Over the years I've probably experimented with more patterns trying to fool front-end *Baetis* risers than anything else. Although I've never come up with a silver bullet, I have come across a few regionally well-known patterns over the years that work well. One, the RS-2, was originated by Rim Chung in the early 1970s on my home river, the South Platte.

RS-2

Hook:	TMC 101 or TMC 100, sizes 16 to 26.
Thread:	Black 8/0 to 14/0 or a color that matches the naturals.
Tail:	Two dark-dun Microfibetts, tied split.
Abdomen:	Natural beaver, or beaver dyed to match the naturals.
Thorax:	Natural beaver, or beaver dyed to match the naturals.

Wing:	Dun or gray fluff from the base of a pheasant feather, or from a dun or brown saddle hackle.

Use the gray "fluff" at the base of a pheasant feather or from a dun or brown saddle hackle for the wing on the RS-2.

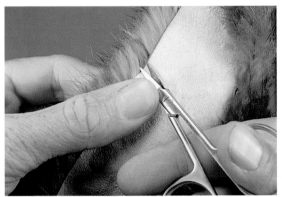

Rim Chung used natural gray beaver for the original RS-2. He prefers cutting it directly from a hide because more color variations are available and it's easier to get the exact amount necessary.

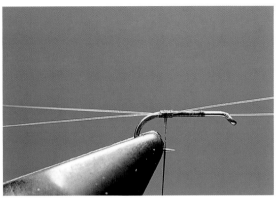

Step 1. Tie in two Microfibetts to make a split tail. Attach one on the far side of the shank with a loose wrap or two of thread, and then attach the second, also loosely, on the near side. Make one wrap of thread beneath both tails to further separate them.

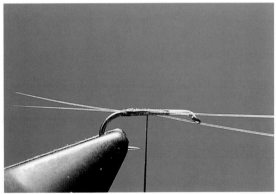

Step 2. Pull the tails through the loose wraps until they are the right length—anywhere from shank length to half again as long. Now secure them in place and clip the excess.

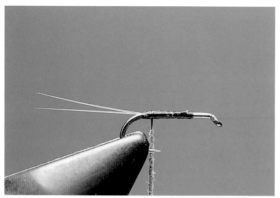

Step 3. Apply a very thin layer of beaver dubbing to the thread. Do not use dubbing wax. Twist the dubbing onto the thread very tightly. Rim Chung actually twists in opposite directions with the thumb and forefinger of both hands to get the dubbing on the thread as tight as possible.

Step 4. Wrap the dubbed thread forward to form the abdomen and the rear half of the thorax. Note that both parts of the body are slender.

Step 5. Cut or strip a clump of fluff from the base of a pheasant-body feather or a saddle hackle. Moisten the tips to make the clump easier to control, and tie it in at the front of the partial thorax.

Step 6. Complete dubbing the thorax, form the head, and tie off.

Step 7. Pull the wing straight up and trim it at an angle as shown.

Rim's elegant pattern is simplicity in action. It accurately represents an emerging *Baetis* nymph or, for that matter, most emerging mayfly nymphs. Although you could probably get away with tying the pattern's required split tails in any of several ways, Rim's technique is worth learning. One dark-dun Microfibett (beaver guard hair was used in the original) is tied in with a couple of loose wraps of thread alongside the far side of a Tiemco TMC 101 hook. Another Microfibett goes along the near side of the shank. Rim then makes one cinch-up wrap *under* the two tails that helps to separate them more. When the tails are positioned correctly he pulls them through the loose wraps to the proper length (shank length to one and a half times as long). He then snugs them in place with a few more thread wraps and cements them.

"It's important that the tails be spread. I have my own notion about how they should be tied. I think the forked tail affects the behavioral charac-

teristics of the fly when it's in the water. It creates a degree of stability, or maybe it turns it upstream. I don't know what it is, but it just seems to make a difference," Rim says.

The body is very tightly dubbed beaver. Rim says he's experimented with synthetics, but finds them more difficult to work with. The original pattern calls for natural gray beaver, which represents the colors of a wide variety of *Baetis* nymphs. Rim prefers beaver cut directly from a hide to packaged fur because there are more color variations to choose from on a hide. It's also easier to consistently measure and remove the very sparse amounts of dubbing critical to the RS-2 design. In recent years, Rim has used dyed beaver to extend the color range of the RS-2.

To achieve the thin, segmented look of the abdomen, Rim applies a very fine portion of beaver dubbing to unwaxed thread and twists it on with the thumb and forefinger of each hand—one hand twists clockwise, the other, counter clockwise. This makes for an extremely thin, tightly dubbed body. Rim believes the translucence of the thin dubbing highlights the thread color underneath, adding life to the imitation. He uses the same dubbing to build the rear half of a thin thorax, adds a wing made from the dun-colored fluff found at the base of a saddle hackle or pheasant feather, and dubs the rest of the thorax before tying off. Rim slightly wets the tips of the fluff before tying it to make it easier to control. The final step is to cut the wing on a slant, forming a short stub.

Rim Chung mainly fishes the RS-2 with short-line dead-drift nymphing tactics before the hatch begins or early on in the hatch. He often uses lifts to give the fly a swimming action. The RS-2 can also be fished very effectively in the surface film when trout are rising. It's extremely effective when fished as a dropper twelve to eighteen inches behind a *Baetis* dry fly. Use a clinch knot at the bend of the hook to attach the dropper. Sometimes the tiniest microshot attached midway between the dry fly and dropper increases the effectiveness of the RS-2.

Rim's explanation of how he came up with the RS-2 is instructive for all fly tiers.

"I was looking at the photographs of the nymph patterns in a catalog. They all had different names and there were lots of them, but the funny thing was they all looked the same. I began to think, why not just develop a single pattern that did what all these others did?" Rim says.

Rim's first attempt was the RS-1, which was essentially a standard nymph pattern tied with a beaver dubbed body, split tails, and a standard wing case. He says that after he came up with the RS-1 he began paying more attention to aquatic insects as they emerged. It occurred to him that if he could make his RS-1 an emerger pattern, its trout-catching abilities would be even broader. That's when he came up with the short fluff wing in place of the wing case. The "RS" means "Rim's Semblance" because the fly isn't meant to imitate any one insect species, but rather is designed to cover a broad spectrum of naturals.

"It works for me," Rim says. It must, because it's the *only* fly pattern he's carried for the past twenty years.

WD-40

The WD-40 is another great fly pattern for early on in the hatch. I learned about it on one of America's great small-fly tailwaters, the San Juan River in northwestern New Mexico. John Flick, a guide and co-owner of Duranglers Flies & Supplies, told me that fly fisher Mark Engler came up with the WD-40 a number of years ago to imitate an emerging blue-winged olive. The fly has a tail of barred mallard flank to imitate a trailing shuck, a thin abdomen made of olive thread, and a mallard-flank wing case. The oversize, globular thorax is made of gray dubbing. Clearly, it's the thorax that triggers trout to strike.

WD-40

Hook:	TMC 2487, TMC 2488, Daiichi 1130, size to match the natural insect.
Thread:	Olive or olive-brown, 8/0 to 14/0.
Tail:	Mallard flank.
Abdomen:	The tying thread.
Wing case:	Mallard flank.
Thorax:	Muskrat or gray synthetic dubbing.

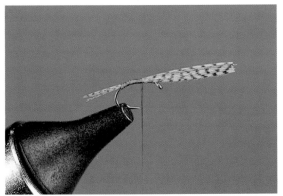

Step 1. Tie in nicely barred mallard-flank fibers to suggest a trailing shuck. Make the abdomen with the tying thread.

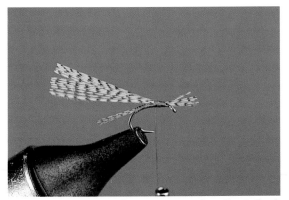

Step 2. Tie in another section of mallard flank for the wing case.

Step 3. Dub the thorax. It should be oversize.

Although the first WD-40s were tied on straight-shank hooks, today most are dressed on continuous-bend models. This fly can be fished in the film as an emerger or dead-drifted as a nymph. Along with the original dressing, the chocolate WD-40 with a chocolate abdomen and thorax is highly effective on the San Juan River.

SOUTH PLATTE QUIGLEY

Another front-end pattern, also well known on the South Platte River, is a variation of a regionally famous California pattern known as the "Quigley." Joe Burke describes the history of the Quigley Cripple in *Tying Flies with Jack Dennis and Friends*. The Quigley Cripple was created by

Step 4. Pull the wing case over the thorax. Tie down the mallard flank, clip the excess, and finish the head.

Californian Bob Quigley after he noticed that a Humpy worked better after it had been chewed up by the trout. Quigley surmised that the damaged Humpy with the splayed deer hair looked like a partially emerged or crippled dun. His original pattern used marabou for a tail and abdomen, deer hair for flotation, and a sparse hackle for added stability. The Quigley has been modified by a number of tiers, and a thin version has found wide acceptance on western tailwaters and spring creeks.

Scott Fraser's South Platte Quigley is a variation tied specifically to imitate *Baetis.* Fraser emphasizes sparseness throughout the pattern. He uses the Tiemco TMC 206BL hook in sizes 18 and 20. Five or six strands of white Z-Lon representing a trail-

ing shuck are tied in just past the bend of the hook so that they are cocked slightly down. Fraser makes the abdomen with olive-brown 6/0 Danville thread that he untwists so that it lies flat and makes a smooth, thin body. He stops the abdomen one and a half or two hook-eye lengths short of the front of the shank, and then makes a tight thorax with Umpqua Superfine Brown Olive dubbing (Fraser actually uses the now-unavailable Spectrum synthetic dubbing, but the Superfine is a close match). At this point he ties in the deer-hair wing. Unlike most Quigley patterns, on which the deer hair is stacked and the fine points of the hair positioned out over the hook eye, Fraser ties in the fine deer hair with the tips pointed back toward the hook bend.

SOUTH PLATTE QUIGLEY

Hook:	TMC 206BL, size 18 or 20.
Thread:	Olive-brown 8/0 to 14/0.
Trailing shuck:	White Z-Lon.
Abdomen:	The tying thread.
Thorax:	Umpqua Superfine Brown Olive dubbing.
Wing:	Fine, bleached coastal deer or fine, bleached elk.
Hackle:	Light blue dun or speckled dun.

Step 2. Dub the thorax. Note the space between the thorax and the eye of the hook; you need this room for the wing.

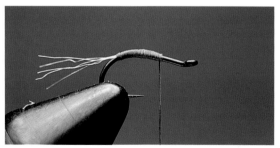

Step 1. Attach five or six strands of white Z-Lon at an angle over the hook bend and trim to length. Wrap the thread forward to make a slim abdomen.

Step 5. Pull the hackle/wing upright; it will splay as it is pulled back. Dub the rest of the thorax in front of the hackle/wing. Tie off.

To tie the Olive Biot Dun, begin by tying in Betts Tailing Fibers to form a forked tail; use three or four fibers per side for a size 16 hook, two fibers per side for size 18 hooks and smaller. Attach an olive goose biot by the tip. Wind the biot so that it forms a smooth body (if you get the rough part of the biot up, just turn it over and wind it the other way) approximately two-thirds the length of the hook shank, and tie it off. Select CDC tips for the hackle/wing (three or four tips for a size 16 fly, two or three tips for sizes 20 and smaller). Measure the hackle/wing to hook-shank length or a little longer. Tie the CDC hackle/wing in about two hook-eye lengths behind the hook eye, butts toward the hook bend, with the natural curve going up. Dub part of the thorax behind the wing. Pull the hackle/wing upright; it will splay as it is pulled back. Dub the rest of the thorax in front of the hackle/wing. Tie off. A topping of mallard or partridge may be added in front of the CDC. Save unused portions of CDC, which can be used on other CDC patterns. CDC stripped from the stem and "bunched" can be used to tie additional Biot Duns. Bunched wings are cut to size after the fly is finished.

The splayed hackle/wing provides excellent flotation.

OLIVE CDC PARACHUTE DUN

Hook: TMC 101, TMC 100, or similar dry-fly hook, sizes 18 to 22.

Thread: Olive 8/0 to 14/0.

Tails: Betts Tailing Fibers or similar synthetic tailing material.

Abdomen: Olive goose biot.

Thorax: Umpqua Gray Olive Superfine dubbing.

Wing post: Polypropylene yarn.

Hackle: Natural dun CDC barbs.

Note: The poly-yarn wing can be white for better visibility on the water or slate gray to match the wing color of the natural. Prepare the wing post before you start to tie. Cut a two-inch-long piece of poly yarn, and split it into pieces of the appropriate thickness. For a typical blue-winged olive imitation you can usually split the poly yarn into four to six sections. Set the pieces of poly yarn aside until needed.

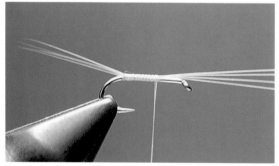

Step 1. Tie in the tailing fibers. Use two fibers per side to make split tails.

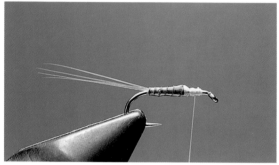

Step 2. Attach the goose biot by the tip and wind it so that it forms a smooth body.

Step 3. Align the butts of two or three CDC feathers.

Step 4. Strip away any short, marabou-like barbs at the bases of the feathers.

Step 5. Stroke the remaining barbs to make them perpendicular to the stems.

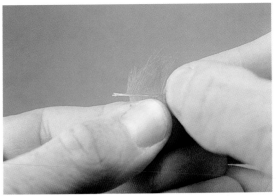

Step 6. Grasp the barbs on one side between your thumb and forefinger. Strip the bundle of barbs from the stem.

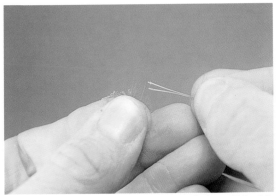

Step 7. Turn the feathers over. While still holding the first bundle between thumb and forefinger, strip the rest of the barbs from the feathers.

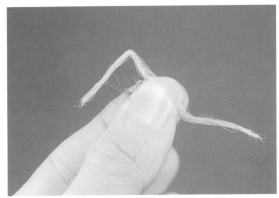

Step 8. Pick up the piece of prepared poly yarn. Put it between your thumb and forefinger, on top of the CDC barbs. You now have a stack of materials—CDC on the bottom, poly yarn on top.

Step 9. Place the CDC-and-yarn stack at an angle across the hook. The yarn must be on top. Make a wrap or two of thread to hold the stack in place.

Step 10. Adjust the stack until it is at right angles to the shank, like a spinner wing. Secure it with a couple of crisscross wraps. Make sure the yarn stays on top.

Step 11. Grab the poly yarn and the CDC fibers, and lift them. Make several wraps around the base of the clump. Let go of the wing and CDC fibers.

Step 12. Dub the thorax.

Step 13. If necessary, poke and twist the CDC to distribute it around the post. Move the CDC out of the way, form the head, and tie off.

Step 14. Stroke the CDC barbs downward and hold them below the hook. Trim them to hook-gap or a bit longer length.

Step 15. The CDC barbs will spring up, forming a nice parachute hackle.

The Olive CDC Parachute Dun is one of my favorite flies for hard-to-catch trout. It floats like a cork and you can see it a mile away on the water. Those are two characteristics that are hard to beat in a small fly. The tails and abdomen are tied the same as those of the CDC Biot Dun.

At first glance, the rest of the CDC Parachute Dun looks like any other parachute pattern. It's natural to conclude that a whole CDC feather has simply been wrapped around the base of the post in the same way that a hackle is wrapped around the post on a standard parachute pattern. Not so. In fact, the stem of a CDC feather will probably break if you try to wrap it around a post. Even if the stem doesn't break, odds are that the uneven lengths of the barbs will force you to trim them anyway.

The trick to making a CDC parachute is to prepare a stack of materials that becomes both the post and the hackle. Stalcup begins the post-and-hackle assembly by matching two CDC feathers at the bases of their stems. Once the bases are aligned, Stalcup holds the feathers by the tips and strokes out the barbs until they are perpendicular to the stems. He strips and discards any short, marabou-like fluff at the very bases of the feathers. Stalcup then grasps all the barbs on

Step 16. Pull the poly yarn straight up. Cut it to hook-shank length.

one side of the feathers between his thumb and forefinger, and strips them from the stems. Without letting go of this first bundle of barbs, Stalcup turns the feathers around, grabs the barbs on the other side of the stems, and strips them off. He ends up with two bunches of CDC barbs grasped between the same thumb and forefinger.

Stalcup then places a two-inch-long piece of polypropylene yarn, which he has prepared ahead of time, in between the tips of his thumb and forefinger. The result is a stack of material with two bundles of CDC barbs on the bottom and the poly yarn on top. The poly yarn is prepared by dividing a standard-size piece into appropriately sized sections for the fly being tied. Most of the time that will be four sections, except on very small flies where less poly is required. When the yarn is divided, Stalcup gives it a twist to form it into a rope.

Stalcup then places the stack on top of the hook shank, taking care to keep the poly on top and the CDC barbs on the bottom. Stalcup has found that the easiest way to attach the stack to the hook is to hold it at an angle to the shank and make a couple of wraps of thread to hold it in place. Once the stack is secured, he pulls the material to a 90-degree angle to the hook shank and makes another wrap or two of thread to form a crisscross. At this point, the stack of materials resembles a spinner wing bound across the hook.

Now comes the neat part. Stalcup gathers the CDC and poly yarn between his thumb and forefinger, pulls it straight up, and makes several wraps around the base. He releases the stack, and then grabs only the poly yarn and twists it a little to dis-tribute the CDC around the base of the post. Then he dubs the thorax and ties off behind the eye.

The final step is to trim the materials. Stalcup gathers all the CDC barbs (but none of the poly yarn) between his thumb and forefinger and pulls them straight down. He cuts the barbs to hook-gap length. They spring back up to form the prettiest parachute hackle you've ever seen. Finally, he trims the poly-yarn post to length.

Although this process sounds complicated, you'll find that it gets easier after a few tries. Initially, you may have trouble stripping the CDC barbs from the stem. The trick is to place your thumb and forefinger over the entire bunch of CDC barbs at one time, clamp down, and strip. Don't try to start at one end of the feather and move down the stem. Don't worry if the bundles aren't neat—you'll trim them anyway. Concentrate on getting them off the stem and making the stack of CDC barbs and poly yarn.

THE SECRET WEAPON

There's another quirky, blue-winged olive pattern that works great in low-water autumn conditions when trout often are difficult to please. I call it my secret weapon and it's so easy to tie that you don't need a recipe or tying instructions. Start with a small 1X-short midge hook (I use a size 24 Tiemco TMC 501) and red 8/0 or finer thread. The pattern consists of a very long, forked Microfibett tail, a Compara-dun–style wing of white Z-Lon (which reduces bulk on tiny hooks), and—here's the real kicker—a body dubbed dirty white! Use fur or synthetic dubbing, as long as it's dirty white.

THE SECRET WEAPON

Hook: TMC 501, TMC 518, sizes 24 to 28.

Thread: Red 10/0 to 14/0.

Tail: White or blue dun synthetic tailing fibers, tied split, one on each side.

Body: Umpqua Blue Dun Superfine dubbing or similar "dirty" white fine, synthetic dubbing.

Wing: White Z-Lon.

Step 3. Dub the body.

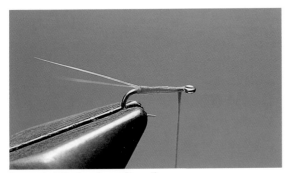

Step 1. Tie in the split tail.

Step 2. Tie in the Z-Lon wing with tips over the hook eye.

Step 4. Pull the wing upright. Make a thread "dam" to hold the wing in place. If necessary, pick and pull the Z-Lon fibers to adjust the wing into a fully splayed configuration. Trim the wing to hook-shank length or a little longer.

Step 5. The finished fly is small enough that it only needs the split tails and splayed Z-Lon wing for flotation.

By most expert accounts, this pattern shouldn't work at all. My fly-colorist friends hate the idea that a white-winged, white-bodied fly can catch trout that are eating naturals that have gray wings and olive or even dark brown bodies. I humor them by observing that maybe the red thread under the thinly dubbed white body suggests a darker fly. But it just might be that I pick up more strikes because the light-colored fly is so much more visible on the water's surface. More intriguingly, perhaps the red-thread head imitates the prominent, red, turbinate eyes of the male *Baetis.* Maybe those red, top-shaped eyes are the trigger. I don't know. I just know that the fly has saved the day for me on numerous occasions and

I honestly don't care why. It's one of those glorious little patterns that doesn't abide by science or reason, but the trout like it.

Along with these "in the film" patterns, I also use traditionally hackled dry-fly patterns for special cases. A. K. Best converted me to his Olive Quill Dun many years ago for fishing heavy riffles or for use on windy days when you want the imitation to bounce and skip over the surface just like the emerging duns. In this situation, an Adams or a tiny Quill Gordon will also often do the trick.

Fishing to trout taking blue-winged olives on or near the top is as good as it gets. Tying these flies is great, but fishing them during the hatch is ecstasy.

CHAPTER TEN

Tiny Parachutes

As the years go by, I find myself sitting around waiting for hatches a lot more than I used to. Most of my sitting takes place on rivers I know well, where I have a pretty good idea which hatches will occur when. If conditions are right, I feel justified waiting for a hatch that *should* come off.

Apparently I'm not the only fly fisher who appreciates sitting around. Several years ago someone constructed a crude bench alongside a pool known as the Duck Pond on a tailwater I frequent. It's a pleasant spot to while away the time and keep in touch with the trout. The bench makes me sit up straight-backed and semi-alert for rises to blue-winged olives, pale morning duns, midges, and the occasional Trico. If I sit on the bank, it's always a struggle not to lie down and fall asleep.

Just last season I was waiting around for the blue-winged olives. I was delighted when the first few came bobbing downstream, followed by the bulges that I've come to know are the trout working over the emergers. On a normal day I would have rigged up immediately with some sort of emerger based on the Pheasant Tail pattern and started casting, but I held my seat on the

bench and calmly tied on a size 20 dry fly. I told myself that I would wait until I saw the first rise to a dun, and then I'd begin fishing. I wanted it to be pure and simple—a single trout rising to a single dry fly, no trailing fly, no droppers. One fly, one trout. The way we used to fish in the good old days.

I chose a classic parachute style of the Blue-Winged Olive to get the job done. I tie it with a hackle-barb tail, goose-biot abdomen, dubbed thorax, folded-barb posted wing of white or gray turkey flat (also known as a turkey T-base feather), and a light dun hackle.

Before long I marked a steadily rising fish just out from the far bank. The moment I saw it take a dun, I got up and positioned myself downstream and across from the trout. It would make a better story if I could say how I agonized through countless casts to get the perfect drift over the fish, but the truth is the trout took the fly on the first cast. Plain and simple. A husky sixteen-inch brown.

I've come to expect that kind of response to parachutes. I've virtually switched over to them from traditionally hackled dry flies for all of my small mayfly-dun imitations. The advantages, especially for picky tailwater and spring creek trout, are overwhelming. The fly sits down in the surface film where it can be taken as a dun or perhaps an emerger, the posted wing has a great silhouette, and most of all I don't have to try to tie little tiny hackle-tip wings. Little tiny hackle-tip wings always have driven me nuts.

In addition, the parachute dry can be trimmed on the stream to make a passable midge imitation (cut down the post), a cripple (trim one side of the hackle so the fly floats on its side), or even a spinner (cut the post and trim the hackle). Simply put, it's a versatile style of dry fly that lends itself to innumerable variations depending on the materials used to tie it. And with a little practice, you'll find tiny parachutes pretty easy to tie.

With that in mind, let's consider tying the Parachute Blue-Winged Olive. In addition to the way I tie the pattern, I've also included several alternative materials and techniques that may be of interest. If you master this Blue-Winged Olive imitation, you'll be well on your way to tying many of the small parachutes. A change in hook size and color produces the Parachute Pale Morning Dun or a Parachute Trico or a match for the tiny mayflies where you fish.

WING MATERIALS AND METHODS

Tying a tiny parachute is essentially the same as tying a larger version. The difference lies in the selection of materials. As it is for all small flies, bulk is the major consideration. This is most crit-ical when selecting materials for the wing and, to a lesser degree, the abdomen. It's possible, though difficult, to make a decent wing on a small fly with calf body hair, but polypropylene or a similar synthetic is the material of choice for many tiers. It's easy to tie and highly visible when the fly is on the water.

Polypropylene is a forgiving wing material for tiers just beginning to work their way down to smaller parachute flies, but you may ultimately want to experiment with fibers from a turkey flat. They make a handsome wing with a good silhouette. I sometimes dye the flat to match the wing color of the natural, but mostly I leave them white for visibility on the water.

I begin tying the parachute-style dry flies at the wing. There are two schools of thought as to where it should be positioned on the hook shank. Some tiers prefer it up close to the hook eye because it makes tying the hackle off a bit less awkward, but traditionally the wing is tied in about one-fourth of the shank length behind the eye. That leaves room to dub a nicely formed thorax around the base of the wing, with space left to tie off the hackle.

The first step in mounting any posted wing is to form a thread base along the hook shank. For wings of synthetic material, cut a one- or two-inch length of material. It should be half the thickness of the desired wing because it will be doubled over in a loop. Comb the synthetic material to separate the fibers.

NO-BULK WING POST

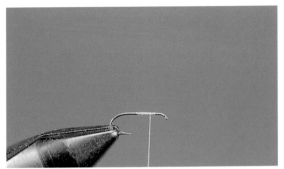

This method lets you make a wing post without adding any bulk to the hook shank. First, wrap a smooth thread base for the wing.

Step 1. With a needle, split a length of poly yarn into pieces half the width of the wings you want to make.

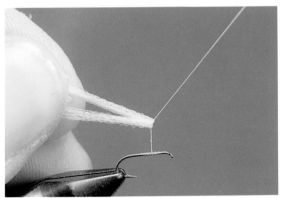

Step 2. Hold the thread vertically above the hook shank. Fold the poly yarn around it as shown.

Step 3. Slide the poly yarn down to the hook. Secure the post with a few wraps of thread in front of and behind it.

Step 4. Wrap the base of the wing to stiffen it and make the foundation for the hackle. This step will make it easier to wrap the feather.

Step 5. If you want to, trim the wing to size. Or you can wait until the fly is completed.

To mount the wing, hold the tying thread vertically above the hook shank, fold the material around the thread, and slide it down to the hook.

An additional wrap can be made over the material to bind it more securely to the hook at this point. Once the poly yarn is secured, post it to a vertical position and make a few wraps in front of the wing and behind it. Several tight wraps of thread are then made horizontally around the base of the wing post to secure it in place. Finally, grasp the top of the wing and wind the thread base up the post three to six more wraps and then down to the bottom again. This will form a base for wrapping the hackle. Some tiers trim the wing to size at this point. On a small fly I usually leave the wing long so I can hold it while winding the hackle, and then I trim it.

BORGER POLY-YARN WING POST

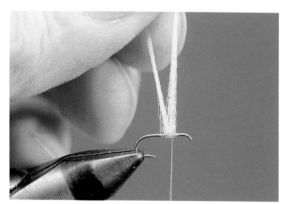

Step 1. Fold the poly yarn around the underside of the hook shank.

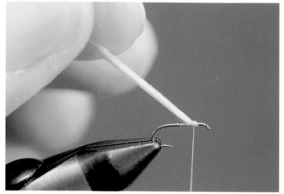

Step 2. Secure the yarn to the hook shank with a few wraps of thread.

Step 3. Wrap the bottom of the post to make a solid base for the hackle.

Step 4. Trim the post to length.

Gary Borger suggests that a synthetic post can also be mounted by folding the yarn around the underside of the hook shank at the thread base and then tilting it toward the rear and taking three or four tight wraps of thread around the material to secure it to the shank. The wing is then lifted to the vertical position where horizontal wraps around the base are made to post it upright.

A TURKEY-FLAT WING—METHOD 1

Turkey flat (also known as turkey T-base) is available in fly shops and through catalogs. Select a turkey-flat feather on which the barbs form a straight edge on each side of the quill.

Step 1. Cut out a section of barbs twice the thickness of the wing you want to make.

Step 2. Align the tips if necessary, and then fold the section lengthwise.

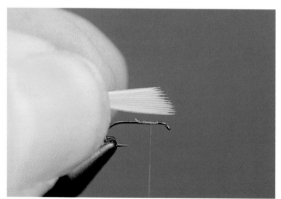

Step 3. Measure the wing along the hook shank. It should be slightly longer than the shank.

Step 4. Pinch the material between thumb and forefinger, and mount the wing with a soft loop.

Step 5. Post the wing upright with wraps of thread in front of it. Wrap the base of the wing to stiffen it.

The turkey-flat wing, or any other wing made of feather barbs, is a bit more involved. For a tiny parachute, I select a turkey flat on which the majority of the barbs extend to the tip of the feather and form a straight edge. Preen the fibers together and cut a single section of barbs from one side of the feather. This section should be double the width of the wing you want to make. Fold it in half to form the wing clump. If the tips aren't perfectly aligned, they can usually be adjusted. The folding method works well for smaller wings that aren't too wide. It's fast and saves material; I can usually get as many as five or six wings out of a single feather.

A TURKEY-FLAT WING—METHOD 2

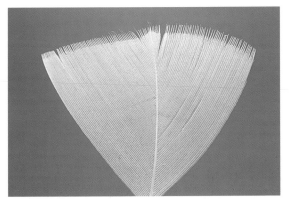

Step 1. Select a turkey flat on which the barbs form a straight edge on each side of the quill.

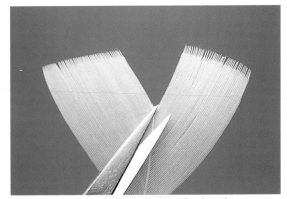

Step 2. Make a notch in the feather by cutting the quill and removing a section of feather. The notch should be at least one and a half times the length of the wing you want to make.

Step 3. Cut the quill to form a V-shaped section of feather that is the width of the desired wing.

Step 4. The V-shaped section of wing.

Step 5. Fold the feather over at the quill. The raised section of quill should be on the *inside* of the fold.

Step 6. Most of the time, when the feather is folded over the tips will nicely align. If they don't, adjust them so they are aligned.

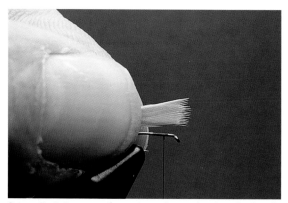

Step 7. Measure the wing along the hook shank. It should be slightly longer than the shank.

Step 8. Post the wing upright with wraps of thread in front of it. Wrap the base of the wing to stiffen it.

An alternative to cutting the wing material from one side of the feather is to cut the feather at the quill to form a V of barbs along either side of it that are the width of the desired wing. The V is then folded over the quill to form the wing, which is mounted in the same way as a wing made from folded-over barbs cut from one side of the feather. You won't get as many wings out of a feather using this alternative, but some tiers prefer how they look and think they are easier to handle.

When mounting a turkey flat wing, remember that it must be sized before it is attached to the hook. I make it a hair longer than the hook shank. Pinch the material between the thumb and forefinger of your left hand at the mounting point, and use a soft loop to tie it in. It's like mounting a quill-slip wing on a wet fly, except the tip of the wing points out over the hook eye rather than back toward the bend. This technique prevents the barbs from rolling together and spoiling the flat silhouette of the wing.

The mounted wing is posted by pulling it up into a vertical position and forming a bump of thread in front of it. Don't worry if some of the barbs separate when you post the wing. They will come together when you make four or five wraps of thread up the bottom of the post to form a base for the hackle. You may have to hold the tip of the wing when making those wraps.

TAILS, BODIES, AND HACKLES

Once the wing is completed, I move to the tail and work my way up the hook shank. In the past I often tied a forked tail of Microfibetts, using one on each side for flies size 20 and smaller and two on each side for size 18 patterns. More recently I've been tying my parachutes with the traditional hackle-barb tail because I think it can pass for either a tail or a trailing shuck. Once the tail is mounted and I've created a smooth, tapered base of thread, I'm ready to mount the abdomen material.

Goose biots and stripped quills are both good choices for abdomens because they reduce bulk, but a finely dubbed abdomen is also suitable. With a goose biot you can form a smooth or ribbed abdomen. I prefer the smooth abdomen.

Shane Stalcup showed me a way to ascertain if the wound biot will be smooth or ribbed before you make the first wrap. The trick is to pull the biot from the stem rather than cut it. You will see a notch on one side at the base. If the notch is toward the rear when the biot is wound, the biot will create a smooth abdomen. If the notch is toward the front, the abdomen will be ribbed. A biot or quill will break less often if you dampen it before winding. The abdomen is wrapped almost to the base of the wing, leaving room for the thorax.

PARACHUTE BLUE-WINGED OLIVE DUN WITH TURKEY-FLAT WING

Hook:	TMC 100 or similar down-eye dry-fly hook, sizes 18 to 22.
Thread:	Olive or gray 8/0 to 14/0.
Tail:	Dun Hoffman Tailing Hackle barbs or dun hackle barbs.
Abdomen:	Olive goose biot.

Thorax:	Umpqua Gray Olive Superfine dubbing.
Wing:	White or gray turkey-flat feather.
Hackle:	Medium dun.

Step 1. Make the turkey-flat wing.

Step 2. Tie in a clump of hackle fibers for the tail, and wrap a smooth, tapered base for the abdomen.

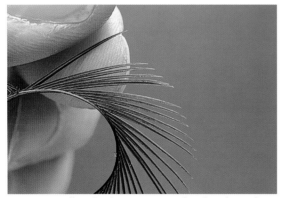

Step 3. Pull—don't cut—a single olive biot from the stem.

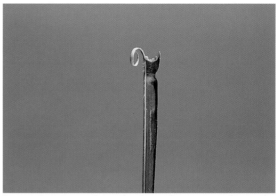

Step 4. Note that the biot has a notch at the base. To make a smooth abdomen, tie in the biot so that the notch faces rearward as you wrap the body. If you tie the biot in with the notch facing toward the front, the body will have a rough rib on it.

Step 5. Tie in the biot with the notch facing the rear of the hook.

Step 6. Wind the biot forward to create a smooth body.

Step 8. Dub the thorax. Don't crowd the eye of the hook; be sure to leave enough room to tie off the hackle.

Step 7. Mount the hackle feather, concave side down, at the base of the wing and then bind the stem of the hackle to the thread base at the bottom of the wing. This will make winding it easier.

Step 9. Wind the hackle clockwise as seen from above. Make each wrap beneath the preceding one.

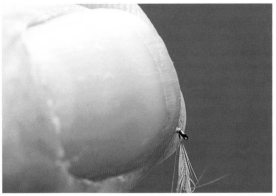

Step 10. Let the hackle pliers hang on the near side of the hook. Carefully gather all the hackle fibers and pull them toward the rear of the hook.

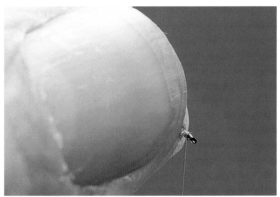

Step 12. Clip the excess feather, form and whip-finish the head.

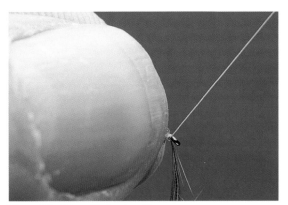

Step 11. Tie off the hackle stem.

Step 13. Let go of the hackle. If necessary, preen and tug the wing and parachute back into their respective positions.

When the abdomen is completed, it's time to mount the hackle. I use a hackle that's a bit larger than one I'd use for a traditional hackle collar. On small flies, I don't get too fancy. I just strip the barbs from the base of the feather and tie it in concave side down near the base of the wing post. Leave enough stripped stem to make a wrap or two up the wing post without flaring any hackle.

After attaching the hackle feather, dub the thorax. Wrap the hackle clockwise (as seen from above) down to the bottom of the post. On a small fly, three wraps will do. Try to keep the concave side of the hackle feather down during the entire process. This prevents flaring. You may have to hold the post in your left hand when you wrap the hackle.

If you have trouble winding the hackle, try wrapping the stripped stem of the hackle up to the top of the thread base on the post. This will prevent the hackle from twisting on the first wrap. Some tiers find that the hackle seats better if they strip a few barbs from the side of the feather that will come into contact with the post on the first wrap. Actually, you can get away with stripping all the barbs from that side of the feather. You don't need much hackle to float a small fly.

Tying off the hackle presents almost as many options as mounting it, but once again I try to keep it simple. After the final wrap of hackle, I give it a little tug to tighten the wraps against the post and seat it. I then pull the hackle pliers straight out to the hook eye, gather up the hackle barbs that project over the hook eye with the thumb and forefinger of my left hand, and tilt them toward the rear. At this point I drape the hackle pliers over the hook shank and let the tool dangle. That frees a hand to tie off the hackle at the eye. After a few more wraps of thread, cut the excess hackle as close as possible and whip-finish the thread.

Things can get a little hectic during this phase, and your hackle pliers might drop to the floor when you cut off the excess hackle, but I just let them go because I want to get the whip-finish on the head before I let go of the fibers with my left hand. If everything works well, you won't have any hackle barbs caught under the thread, but if you do they can be trimmed.

When you release the hackle from your left hand, it typically comes right back into place. If it doesn't, you may need to pull the post back up to the vertical position, reposition a few hackle barbs with a tug here and there, or both.

THE BEATTY HACKLE METHOD

Step 1. Tie the fly the same as you did for the Parachute Blue-Winged Olive Dun with Turkey-Flat Wing. When you dub the thorax, stop with the thread hanging just in front of the wing.

Step 3. Hold the thread horizontally toward the rear. Make three to five wraps *between* the hackle tip and the bottom wrap of hackle. This will secure the hackle to the base of the wing.

Step 2. Wind the hackle clockwise, looking down on the fly. Hold the hackle toward the rear of the fly and slightly below horizontal.

Step 4. Trim the leftover feather. Use a half-hitch tool (an old bobbin with a tapered metal tube as shown here works well for small flies) to tie off the thread behind the hook eye.

Step 5. Slide the half-hitch tool over the eye of the hook.

Step 6. Slip the half-hitch onto the shank and tighten it.

Step 7. Make a few more half-hitches, tighten them, and clip the thread.

If gathering the hackle barbs in your left hand and tilting them back drives you crazy, you might want to consider a tie-off technique that Al Beatty showed me several years ago. Mount the hackle the same way I described, but when you dub the thorax, finish with the thread at the base of the wing post. Wind the hackle down the post as previously described, but when you get to the bottom, hold the hackle tip with the pliers toward the tail of the fly and a bit lower than horizontal. Now make a thread wrap between the hackle tip and the lowest wrap of hackle. This binds the hackle stem to the post. Make several more wraps around the base to firmly secure the hackle stem to the post. Cut off the excess hackle and bring the tying thread straight out from the post to the hook eye. A half-hitch tool (I use an old bobbin) is then used to make four or five half-hitches at the hook eye without having to lift the hackle. You may want to cement or lacquer the half-hitches, but I don't always do it and the flies still hold up well.

Although tying the tiny parachute may be a little cumbersome at first, it will, with practice, become faster and easier than traditionally hackled dry flies. It's worth the effort, too. Tiny parachutes have many applications and can be tied in almost infinite variations. You won't regret having them in your fly box.

CHAPTER ELEVEN

Tricos

Fly fishers' feelings toward the genus of tiny mayflies known as *Tricorythodes,* or Tricos or trikes in angler lingo, have ranged from indifference to anger. To this day there are anglers who will not admit that Trico hatches and spinner falls are fishable at all. For those fly fishers, the dry-fly season ends when hatches of larger mayfly species trail off in early summer.

Other anglers refer to Tricos, which are characterized by oversize white wings that are out of proportion to the insects' short, chunky bodies, as "the white curse." The epithet is easy to understand after you've spent a couple of strikeless hours casting to one trout after another that is busily sipping, or sometimes literally gulping, the thousands of spent Trico spinners that can end up on the water after an early morning mating swarm. I've had days when the Trico spinner fall made me wonder if I ever knew how to fish a dry fly in the first place.

Actually, many of the misunderstandings about Tricos have their root in the insects' unique biology and small size. Vince Marinaro called them the "hidden hatch" because unless the light is right it is difficult to see the tiny duns on the water or the spinners darting about in mating swarms over it.

Tricos range in size from 3 to 6 millimeters in length, with those in the eastern United States appearing to be somewhat smaller than their western counterparts. The nymphs thrive in the silt at the tails of pools, in tailwater environments, spring creeks, and some lake environments. Just a small amount of silt between, over, or under streambed rubble will support large numbers of trikes. I once put three small, slightly silt-covered rocks from Colorado's South Platte River into a ten-gallon aquarium. When the insects hidden on those rocks hatched a few weeks later, I counted forty-two Tricos. The point here is that given the right habitat, Tricos often hatch in huge numbers and provide a significant source of food to the trout.

TRICO BIOLOGY

In terms of biology, the *Tricorythodes* are unique. After hatching, their life cycle is one of the most rapid among the mayflies. Typically, the males hatch throughout the night, and females hatch early in the morning. Both sexes molt very quickly into spinners and can often be seen in mating swarms over the water by eight in the morning. Spent males may fall to the surface within the next few hours. The females are close behind them, falling to the water after depositing their fertilized eggs.

For years anglers thought that the Trico duns actually molted in the air while making their quick switch from dun to spinner. Fred Arbona Jr. disagrees. In *Mayflies, the Angler, and the Trout,* Arbona states that "the mechanics of a dun metamorphosing to a spinner would undoubtedly require that it must do so at rest."

Arbona explains that anglers assumed the Tricos molted in midair because the females, which hatch much later than the males, often take off into the swarms of hovering males before they become fully detached from their dun exoskeletons. Most seasoned Trico-hatch fishers have a story or two about these exoskeleton shucks fluttering down from the sky like a light summer snow, making it easy to believe that molting occurs in the air.

Angler interest in Tricos has traditionally been focused on the spinner fall, during which the water is sometimes blanketed with spent spinners. The incredible abundance of bugs brings even the largest trout to the surface. Since the spinner fall often occurs over slower water, it can make for an extremely selective rise of trout.

Over the past few decades anglers have realized that if they arrive early in the day, when the female duns are hatching, they can have some excellent fishing. Even more recently, the value of nymph patterns has been noted. That makes sense: It's not uncommon to find trout taking Trico nymphs, duns, and spent spinners, all before noon.

I've gone through a number of phases both fishing Trico patterns and tying them. Initially, I painstakingly matched male and female duns along with male and female spent spinners. I found that at times the thick-bodied, olive-hued females in either the dun or spinner form might be more effective. At other times, imitations of the darker, thinner male turned the trick. When I finally realized that a nymph could make a good trailer fished behind a dun or spinner imitation, I matched it with a simple, black biot-body dressing. Later I added an olive-brown fur pattern to my nymph assortment.

Over time I found myself getting a little lazy during the Trico hatch. I drifted into carrying only dark-bodied dun and spinner imitations. I didn't catch as many trout during the spinner fall, but I didn't need to change flies as often, either.

Some of that laziness may have come from living in the West. Our Tricos are a bit larger, and I believe our trout are less picky during the hatch. An expedition to southeastern Pennsylvania's Falling Springs and Big Spring creeks set me straight. The sophisticated Pennsylvania trout didn't want anything to do with my big, clunky western facsimiles.

Along with some much needed humiliation, the Pennsylvania trip demonstrated to me that the southeastern part of that state is the real cradle of Trico fishing and Trico fly patterns. Legendary anglers such as Vincent Marinaro and Charlie Fox were among the first to believe that trout could be consistently landed on artificial flies during the Trico hatch. Marinaro's article on Tricos in a 1969 issue of *Outdoor Life* was among the first to bring the tiny mayflies to the attention of a growing number of fly fishers.

Bob Miller uses a modification of Chauncy Lively's wonder wing for his Trico imitations. Pictured here are a female spinner (left) and a male spinner.

BOB MILLER'S TRICOS

Miller uses a dun hen saddle to make wings.

To begin a wing, reverse the barbs on the hen saddle, stroking them toward the butt of the feather and pinching them in that position.

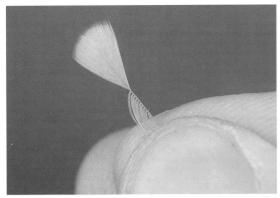

Strip away the barbs on one side of the quill. Cut off the tip of the feather (still present in this photo), and attach the wing at the butt end.

A more recent contribution from Pennsylvania is Bob Miller's *Tricos: A Practical Guide to Fishing and Tying* Tricorythodes *Imitations and Related Patterns* (Rodcrafters Press, Inc., Allentown, PA, 1997). It's a highly detailed, delightful book containing fly patterns and fishing techniques that apply to Trico nymphs, duns, and spinners. Miller rightly places equal importance on fly pattern and presentation.

Miller's dun and spinner patterns revolve around a refinement of the "wonder wing," which is generally credited to fly tier Chauncy Lively. The wonder wing is made by stroking the barbs of a rooster or hen hackle back (toward the butt, that is) and holding them against the stem. The result looks very much like the wing of a mayfly or caddisfly. I used the wonder wing on caddis patterns in the mid-1970s, but like many anglers I forgot about it after a few years. Miller modified Lively's wing for use on small flies by using thin-stemmed hen saddle with the barbs on one side of the feather stripped away. The result is a realistic and relatively easy-to-tie wing for both duns and spinners. An extra benefit is that the wing can be easily shortened if you tie it in a bit too long—simply clip away one barb at a time.

The wonder wing is quite durable, with one exception. If the teeth of a hooked trout get into

the wing it can tear out the barbs. Miller repairs the damage by clipping out the loose barbs with small scissors.

Although Miller pays close attention to body dimensions (fat for females, slimmer for males) and color, his main emphasis is on wings. Any angler who has seen Tricos knows that one of these insects appears to be *all* wings. Closer examination is required to see the diminutive, stout body.

It has been my habit over the years to carry Trico spent-spinner imitations with a variety of wing styles. I've often found that if one imitation doesn't do the trick, another might.

To a lesser degree, I use the same strategy with dun imitations. I may carry two or three wing styles that range from traditional hackle-tip wings to posts, cut wings, CDC, and Comparadun variations.

The rest of the fly doesn't vary much. I tie split Microfibett tails (I used to tie the "species correct" three tails seen on the naturals, but have long since gotten over that obsession). I use stripped hackle quill or thread for the abdomen. A cream or olive-cast quill is my favorite for female Trico imitations. For males, stripped peacock, dark olive biot, or black thread gets the job done. I use a black, superfine synthetic dubbing or black beaver for the thorax.

Various small-fly hooks are suitable for Trico imitations. Bob Miller likes the Tiemco TMC 501. Other options might include straight-eye hooks such as the Daiichi 1640, Daiichi 1480, and the old standby Tiemco TMC 101. The Daiichi 1110 or similar light-wire hooks with oversized eyes are sometimes helpful on tiny flies. As a rule, I prefer straight-eye hooks for Trico spinner imitations, but the slightly down-eye, short-shank Partridge K1A can be useful, as is the Tiemco TMC 500U up-eye hook.

WINGS FOR TRICO SPINNERS

With all of this in mind, it may be useful to review techniques and materials that are best suited

The Bob Miller Trico series covers every stage of the insect's life. From left to right, these are the nymph, female dun, male dun, male spinner, female spinner, and knotted or mating pair.

Wing materials account for the most obvious differences among Trico patterns. From left to right, these are Lynn Allison's Organza Trico Spinner, Roger Hill's Hackle-Wing Spinner, a pattern with Krystal Flash wings, one with poly-yarn wings, and a Marinaro-style spinner.

for the winging of Trico imitations, particularly spinners. In most cases, the small size of Trico imitations precludes any fancy tying techniques for the wings. Most often they are attached with X-wraps or a variation of them. Subtle differences in materials and fly presentation are what usually make the difference with Tricos.

Polypropylene and other bright synthetics. More Trico spent-spinner wings are tied with "poly" than any other material. And as Bob Miller writes, they work pretty well at the start of the hatch in July. But the trout do catch on to them. Nonetheless, everyone probably has a poly-winged Trico spinner imitation in his fly box. It's a simple tie. Just X-wrap a length of polypropylene at a right angle to the hook shank. The key is to keep it sparse.

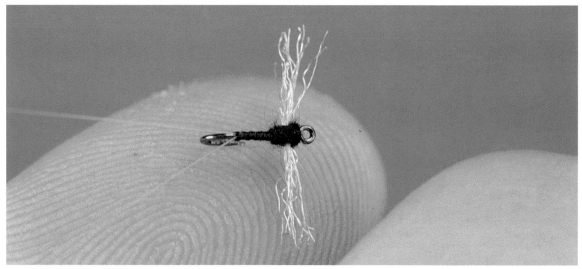

The polypropylene or Antron wing is the most common type used on Trico spinner patterns.

TYING POLY-WING TRICOS

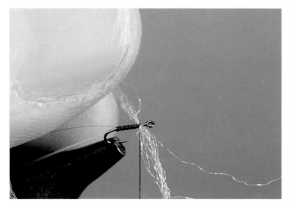

Attach a poly-yarn or Antron wing by simply X-wrapping it in place. Here, the thread forms the first half of the X as it passes diagonally across the wing material.

The second half of the X-wrap is made when the tying thread passes diagonally from the front to the rear. Another X or two will stabilize the wing and improve its durability.

You can alter the standard poly wing a bit by using Antron or white Z-Lon. It's a bit flashier. I prefer the straight Z-Lon, but the newer kinkier material also works.

Lynn Allison, a talented Colorado fly tier, makes a synthetic-wing Trico spinner variation out of the organza material often used to trim wedding dresses. Organza is a bright, flashy nylon

Cover the X-wraps with a fine natural or synthetic dubbing.

woven with the strands at right angles to each other. Allison cuts a small square of the material and removes all the strands going in one direction. This leaves a small bunch of parallel strands, which he X-wraps to the hook. A few wraps of thread around the base of each wing flare the material. The resulting wing is more rigid than poly or Z-Lon and has a pleasing natural appearance.

LYNN ALLISON'S ORGANZA TRICO SPINNER

Hook:	TMC 500U, size 18 or smaller.		Thorax:	Spirit River Black Trico dubbing.
Thread:	Black 8/0 to 14/0.		Thorax overtop:	Black goose biot.
Tails:	White Microfibetts.		Wing:	Organza fibers.
Abdomen:	Moose mane.			

Lynn Allison's Organza Trico Spinner.

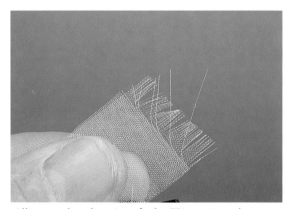

Allison makes the wings for his Trico spinner by picking apart a small piece of organza fabric.

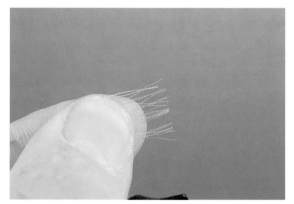

Once the organza is picked apart, the fibers are aligned and then used as wing material.

Allison uses split Microfibetts for the tails, a single moose hair for the abdomen, and black Spirit River superfine dubbing for the thorax, which he finishes with a black goose biot pulled over the top.

Hackle. Before polypropylene, there was hackle, and spent wings created from hackle were

the most common. A number of Trico variations begin with a white, cream, or light dun hackle that is wound around the hook shank in the traditional manner.

The simplest way to make a spent spinner from a traditional dry-fly hackle is to cut the hackle on the top and bottom, leaving wings projecting from the sides of the fly. This technique will work on very small flies, but the resulting wing tends to be quite sparse because the small hook doesn't allow for many turns of

hackle in the first place. When you trim them down into spent wings, there may not be much left.

MARINARO-STYLE TRICO SPINNERS

Step 1. Vince Marinaro found a way to turn a wrapped hackle into spinner wings. Make four or five turns of hackle, then a final wrap through the middle of the collar to splay the fibers. After tying off the hackle, pass the thread under the hackle on the far side of the hook.

Step 3. Now bring the thread forward under the hook shank, gathering the fibers on the near side of the hook. Make a wrap of thread around the shank. The attitude of the wings can be adjusted by applying gentle tension to the tying thread.

Step 2. At the rear of the hackle, loop the thread over the top of the hook shank and bring it toward you.

Step 4. Complete the spent wings with a few X-wraps to pull down the fibers above the shank.

Step 5. Dub a thorax of black beaver or a fine synthetic dubbing material.

Vince Marinaro found a way to use all of the hackle to make spinner wings. His technique requires a fair degree of dexterity. Make four or five wraps of hackle, taking care that they're not too close together. Make the final wrap through the center of the other wraps, and then tie it off at the front. This flares the hackle. Now comes the tricky part. Bring the thread directly under the hook shank toward the rear, and use the thread to pick up half the hackle; that is, the thread catches and lifts the hackle fibers beneath the far side of the hook. At the rear of the hackle, bring the thread up on the far side of the shank and loop it over the top of the shank toward you.

Bring the thread forward again, this time under the near side of the hook shank. This maneuver picks up the rest of the hackle fibers. At the front of the hackle, bring the thread up and make a wrap around the shank. You have used the thread to catch and lift all the fibers beneath the hook.

Obviously, you have to make these maneuvers with almost no tension on the thread. After you've lifted all the hackle, pulling on the thread—*carefully*—will adjust the height to which the fibers are lifted. Repeating the entire procedure firms up the wings. Once you're done with the fibers below the hook, you can complete the spent wings by splitting the hackle above the hook with a few X-wraps.

It takes a bit of practice to learn to gather up the hackle on the bottom, but Marinaro felt it was worth the effort. He also suggested that a more simple, fully spent version of the fly can be rendered by tying in two pieces of a thorax material, such as peacock herl, on the top and the bottom of the hook shank, winding the hackle, and then dividing the fibers into a spent-wing configuration by pulling each strand of herl forward and through the hackle, and then tying each one off.

DATUS PROPER–STYLE SPENT TRICO SPINNER

Hook:	TMC or Daiichi dry-fly hook, size 18 or 20.
Thread:	Black 8/0 to 14/0.
Tails:	Long dun hackle barbs or Microfibetts.
Wing:	White hackle wrapped over the front two-thirds of hook, then trimmed on the bottom.
Body:	Black dubbing. Wind the dubbed thread through the hackle.

Author and fly tier Datus Proper winds the hackle over the front two-thirds of the hook, and then dubs a wisp of black fur or synthetic through it for reinforcement. The bottom of the hackle is then trimmed. Proper's "half-hackle" wing makes the fly considerably more visible on the water and is quite durable.

The Datus Proper–style spent Trico spinner.

ROGER HILL'S HACKLE-WING TRICO SPINNER

Hook: Tiemco TMC 100, sizes 18 to 26.
Thread: Black 8/0 to 14/0.
Tails: Two dun Microfibetts.
Abdomen: Tying thread coated with head cement.
Thorax: Black fur.
Wing: Hackle fibers.

Roger Hill, the author of a fine guide to fishing Colorado's South Platte River, ties a very sparse spinner using eight non-webby barbs cut from a grizzly or dun rooster neck. He aligns four of the barbs with the tips going in one direction and lays the other four on top of them with the tips going in the opposite direction. He then carefully ties the barbs to the hook shank with X-wraps. The wings are then trimmed to shank length and pushed up, causing them to flare. A few wraps of thread using very light tension are then made through the barbs to hold them in place. Wing position can be adjusted by altering thread tension slightly to flare the wings.

Hackle tips. Hackle tips also make effective spent spinner and dun wings. The best come from more webby, broader hen necks or hen saddles. White, cream, or dun is best.

Cul-de-canard. These wings are easy to tie. Simply cut an appropriate amount of white or dun CDC from the stem and fasten the material to the shank with X-wraps. Either cut or tear the CDC to the proper length. The effect and visibility of the wing can be enhanced by adding a strand of pearlescent pearl Krystal Flash over the top of the CDC.

Roger Hill's Hackle-Wing Trico Spinner.

A. K. Best uses entire hen-neck feathers to make Trico wings. From left to right, these are his male Trico spent spinner, Parachute Trico Dun (turkey flat is used for the post), and a traditionally hackled Trico dun with oversize hen-hackle wings.

CDC TRICO SPENT SPINNER

Hook: Any dry-fly hook, sizes 18 to 26.
Thread: Black 8/0 to 14/0.
Tails: White or dun Microfibetts.
Body: Black thread; may be coated with head
           cement.
Wing: White or dun CDC barbs, with one
           strand of pearlescent Krystal Flash on
           top.

The CDC Trico Spent Spinner.

Other synthetics. An array of synthetics such as Zing wing, Krystal Flash, or Stalcup's Medallion Sheeting can be used as Trico spinner wings. Simply X-wrap the material to the hook shank. If you have trouble attaching wider wing material to the shank, twist it to make the attachment point in the center thinner. All-synthetic patterns may not float as long as those that combine materials such as CDC with a synthetic, but a modern fly floatant applied to the body of the fly will float it long enough to see if the trout want to eat it.

DROWNED TRICO SPINNERS

An outfitter I worked for when I was guiding on Colorado's South Platte River had one simple rule: Guides don't fish. That meant that once I got my sports on the water and had them fishing, there was plenty of time for trout watching.

The best trout watching of the season occurred when the Tricos were on. If we got on the water early enough, we could watch the whole pageant unfold. The duns came off, formed into mating swarms over the water, and finally the spinners fell spent to the surface. I always looked forward to the spinner fall because I could be sure there would be plenty happening on top. It was during the spinner fall several years ago that fellow guide Gary Willmart showed me a twist that had escaped me during my years of trout watching. He led me to a rock weir where the water fell a foot or so into the plunge pool below.

"Look," he said as he pointed to the clear water just past the foam created by the falling water. There were trout flashing and darting everywhere.

"Holy cow!" I excitedly replied. Gary motioned me to come upstream to the flat water just above the weir. There were spent Trico spinners all over the surface. He then explained that the spinners were being washed over the weir where the force of the descending water sank them in the plunge pool below. The trout were feasting on the sunken spinners. Gary explained that for the past two weeks he had been fishing his sports below the weir using a two-fly, dead-drift nymphing rig with a poly-wing Trico spent-spinner pattern on the point. It was supposed to be a dry fly, but the trout didn't care. They took the "drowned" Trico with reckless abandon. I quickly followed Gary's example on my guided trips and the sports couldn't have been happier.

The discovery of the trout below the weir motivated me to more closely observe trout rising to Trico spinners elsewhere on the river, and I came to the surprising conclusion that many of them were actually feeding below the surface. As many as half the riseforms I observed weren't the classic dimples of trout taking spent spinners from the surface, but rather the head-to-tail porpoising rises or mound-type rises of trout feeding below the surface. It made sense that some of the spent spinners would sink and that the trout would feed on them.

Once I realized that the naturals were sinking, it occurred to me that maybe the tiny artificials I was fishing might also be sinking. That would account for the strikes that I often got when I couldn't see the fly. I also realized that for my style of fishing I was going to need a drowned Trico imitation that didn't require putting a split shot on the leader. There was already one candidate for the job in my fly box, too. It was a sparsely tied, commercially available imitation that I'd bought from a fly shop years before. I hadn't used the fly much because I couldn't see it

on the water, but it had proved highly effective when fished as the point fly on nymphing rigs.

The fly's design was simple. It was tied on a Tiemco TMC 100 hook. The forked tail was tied with two white synthetic tailing fibers. The black body was made of thread and the thorax was black synthetic dubbing. The wings were the key to a sinking design. They were simply three pieces of pearlescent Krystal Flash tied across the hook shank to represent splayed, spent wings. Whether intended by the pattern's designer or not, the sparse Krystal Flash wings and slim thread body allowed the fly to break through the surface tension more easily than imitations tied with buoyant polypropylene, hackle fiber, or hackle-point wings.

I made a few modifications to the fly that helped it sink even better. I substituted a size 20, Tiemco TMC 2488H hook for the dry-fly hook. The TMC 2488H is a 2X-heavy, 2X-short, and 3X-wide hook. The heavy wire sinks the fly, the 2X-short shank allows you to tie a fly that looks small, and the 3X-wide gap gives you better hookups. Finally, I changed the thorax from the synthetic material to beaver fur, mainly because I prefer its dubbing characteristics for this pattern.

DROWNED TRICO

Hook:	TMC 2488H, size 20.
Thread:	Black Gudebrod 10/0.
Tail:	Two or three white synthetic tailing fibers.
Abdomen:	The tying thread.
Thorax:	Black beaver fur.
Wings:	Three strands of pearlescent Krystal Flash.

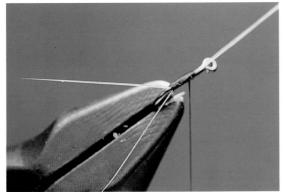

Step 1. Tie in two or three tails and divide them. Wrap a smooth thread abdomen.

Step 2. Tie three strands of Krystal Flash perpendicular to the hook shank with X-wraps.

Step 3. Separate the Krystal Flash strands by wrapping tying thread between them.

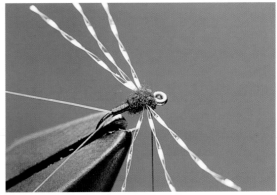

Step 4. Dub the thorax.

Step 5. Trim the wings to the proper length.

I cast this fly to riseforms the same way I fish a floating spent-spinner imitation. The leader can be greased twelve to eighteen inches above the fly and watched to detect the strike. You can also fish the fly as a dropper behind a Trico dun imitation or an easy-to-see Elk Hair Caddis if the trout aren't too spooky. The dry fly will act as a strike indicator when a trout takes the drowned Trico. The Krystal Flash wings actually seem to attract the trout's attention better below the surface than on top.

The drowned Krystal Flash spinner worked well for fish close to the surface in slower water, but I also wanted an imitation that would sink a little quicker. I experimented with beadheads, but couldn't come up with a design I liked. Eventually, I turned to Wapsi Fly's Ultra Wire. The small size Ultra Wire (34 gauge) is perfect for creating a nice segmented body *and* it adds enough weight to get the fly down. Best of all, the wire comes in black, olive, golden olive, and chartreuse. This means you can tie the black-bodied male spinners and olive-bodied female spinners.

I tied a few of the wire-body drowned Tricos with a chartreuse wire abdomen to test if the bright color might be a feeding trigger and found them to be surprisingly successful. I can't say for certain if I discovered a trigger or if this is just another affirmation of the time-honored saying, "It ain't no use without chartreuse." But I can say that I had trout turning out of their feeding lanes to take the fly on several occasions.

My favorite hook for the wire-body version of the drowned Trico used to be the TMC 2457 because the 2X-heavy wire guaranteed that the fly would sink fast, but there was a drawback. The TMC 2457 is only available down to size 18. Tiemco makes the TMC 2488H down to size 24. Even with the extra weight of the wire body, if you go smaller than a size 20 hook you may not be able to get enough wraps of it around the shank to add the weight necessary to immedi-

Small Wapsi Ultra Wire (34 gauge) is perfect for making drowned Trico imitations. Try chartreuse, olive, and black.

ately sink the fly, but it will go down after it drifts a short distance. Very small versions of the fly will sink quicker if you use a fluorocarbon tippet.

I use Gudebrod 10/0 black thread to tie in a forked tail using two or three white synthetic tailing fibers. Once the tails are attached, bring the thread forward to the thorax area. Now it's time to wrap the Ultra Wire abdomen. I don't tie in the Ultra Wire and then wrap forward over it because that creates too much bulk. Instead, I leave a "tag" of wire to hold on to when I make

the first wrap at the tail and then tightly wrap the wire forward. I trim the wire at the rear and the front of the abdomen as close to the hook as possible and crimp it tight against the shank. I use tweezers to crimp the wire. My friend Terry Imlay recommends a dentist's tool. Whatever you use, strive to crimp the wire ends down tight. I don't lacquer the wire body, but you can if you are concerned that the wire will unravel or move. Finish the fly with Antron wings tied spent and a black beaver-fur thorax.

WIRE-BODY DROWNED TRICO

Hook:	TMC 2457, size 18; TMC 2488, sizes 20 to 22.
Thread:	Black Gudebrod 10/0.
Tail:	Two or three white synthetic tailing fibers.
Abdomen:	Black, olive, golden olive, or chartreuse Wapsi Fly Ultra Wire (small).
Thorax:	Black beaver fur.
Wings:	Antron.

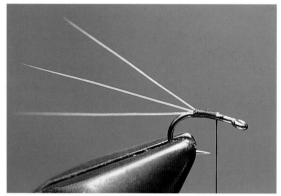

Step 1. Tie in two or three tails and divide them. Wrap a smooth thread base over the back two-thirds of the hook shank.

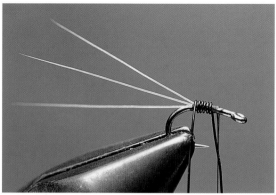

Step 2. Wind Wapsi Ultra Wire around the hook shank to form the abdomen. Note that the wire is not tied to the hook shank. Simply wind it tightly around the shank, trim it at both ends, and crimp the ends close to the hook shank. This method of attaching wire to small hooks helps reduce bulk.

Step 3. Tie Antron wing material perpendicular to the hook shank with X-wraps.

Step 4. Form the thorax and whip-finish the head.

The only way to find the spent-spinner Trico patterns that work on your home waters is to experiment with materials. And keep in mind that one material may provide just the trigger the trout are looking for one day, but be worthless the next. That's when it pays to pack an alternative.

CHAPTER TWELVE

Floating Nymphs

A number of years ago, I was fishing the early spring blue-winged olive hatch on a favorite western tailwater. The locals consider it the first "official" hatch of the season, though we can always expect sporadic hatches of midges throughout the winter and spring. We tend to ignore the midges when the olives come off, not so much because the trout lose interest in them, but more because the olives are the seasonal event signaling the end of winter.

It's a little like when a top-notch, out-of-town blues band comes to town and you forgo visiting your friendly neighborhood bar to listen to the local band. You *know* the local band will still be there, but if you miss the out-of-towners you could end up waiting a year or more before they come back through your neighborhood. That's the way it is with the blue-winged olive hatch.

Unfortunately, knowing that the first official hatch of the season had arrived did little to soothe me on that particular spring morning. Things were not going well. As delighted as I was to see the olives on the water and the rising trout, I could not buy a strike. I worked through my sizable arsenal of blue-winged olive dry flies,

starting with a general-purpose size 20 Adams. When that didn't work I went to a Parachute Adams of the same size, and then dropped down to a size 22. After the trout ignored those flies, it turned into a free-for-all of different patterns: an A. K. Best–style olive quill parachute, a modified Quill Gordon, the incomparable Compara-dun, which almost never fails in small sizes, and even a Griffith's Gnat. I was exhausted by the time I'd tied on, carefully presented, failed to get a strike with, and ultimately cut off all those patterns. My 6X tippet, which had started at about thirty inches long, was down to eight inches.

I found myself in that anxious state of mind that overcomes an angler when he realizes that he's spent the last hour furiously changing flies without success and that the hatch may very well go off without a single strike. It's the same kind of feeling you get when you realize you're lost in the forest and you catch yourself walking faster and faster. Experts say that's the time to sit down on a log and get hold of yourself. And that is what I did, although it might have been due more to mental exhaustion than an understanding that I was "lost" deep in a hatch of blue-winged olives.

I did manage to regain my composure after ten or fifteen minutes of contemplation. And, mercifully, the hatch was still on. That's when I decided that it might not hurt to get downstream of the rising trout and seine the river. It didn't take long for me to realize that there were more than duns on the surface. For every dun that showed up in the screen, there were three or four emerging nymphs. A quick survey told me that many of the emerging nymphs were actually floating on the surface or just under it. A more studied look at the rising trout revealed a telling clue. Most of the duns floating serenely on the water's surface were *not* disappearing down the gullets of fish.

I'd fallen into the classic trap. Rather than take a few minutes to observe what was going on when I first spotted the rising trout, I simply assumed they were taking duns and tied on a dry fly. It's one of the most basic fly-fishing errors. More than anything else, our sport is one of observation, and that's especially true when it comes to fishing small flies.

BLUE-WINGED OLIVE FLOATING NYMPH

Hook:	Standard dry-fly hook, sizes 18 to 24.
Thread:	Olive, size 8/0 or finer.
Tail:	Medium blue dun hackle barbs.
Body:	Umpqua Gray Olive Superfine dubbing or olive beaver.
Thorax:	Umpqua Gray Olive Superfine or olive beaver.
Dubbing ball:	Gray polypropylene dubbing.
Hackle:	Medium blue dun one size smaller than normal, tied parachute style.

Step 2. Dub a tapered body.

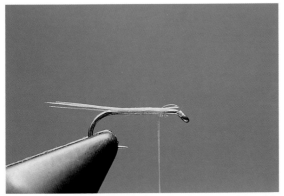

Step 1. Start the thread and tie on several hackle barbs for the tail.

Step 3. Apply a narrow strand of gray polypropylene dubbing to the thread.

Step 4. Roll and compress the dubbing between your fingers to create a tight ball.

Step 5. Position the tying thread and ball above the hook shank.

Step 6. Slide the dubbing ball down to the hook shank.

Step 7. Secure the dubbing ball to the hook shank with a few wraps of thread in front of it and behind it and then a few wraps around its base.

Step 8. Attach the hackle with the shiny side up.

Step 9. Dub the thorax.

Step 10. Wind the hackle around the base of the dubbing ball.

That's when I remembered a little Blue-Winged Olive Floating Nymph that a guide had given me during the hatch several seasons earlier. He'd said it was "dynamite." The size 22 fly had a sparse blue-dun hackle tail, a tapered dubbed body, and an oversized ball of slate-gray polypropylene dubbing fixed squarely on top of the thorax. The Floating Nymph looked easy to tie, so I'd made up a few when I got home and placed them in an obscure corner of my nymph box.

I quickly tied on a new section of 6X tippet and rummaged through my fly box to find the nymphs. After five or six casts, a trout rose confidently to the imitation and I was saved. More important, I had learned the value of the floating nymph.

FLOATING-NYMPH VARIATIONS

If I had been more attentive when I read *Tying the Swisher-Richards Flies,* I would have been aware of the virtues of floating nymphs. Swisher and Richards introduced a split-tail, dubbed-body pattern that had what they called a "stacked" wing case of polypropylene or fur. The wing case is formed by spinning a tight ball of dubbing on the tying thread and sliding the ball into position on the top of the fly. The ball of dubbing keeps the nymph afloat on the surface or in the film. Swisher and Richards started using their Floating Nymph after studying the stomach contents of a number of trout they thought were

Step 11. Tie off and clip the excess hackle.

Floating nymphs are excellent imitations of small, emerging mayflies. From left to right, these examples are a Pheasant-Tail Parachute Floating Nymph, No-Hackle Pheasant-Tail Floating Nymph, No-Hackle Blue-Winged Olive Floating Nymph, and Blue-Winged Olive Parachute Floating Nymph.

The Pheasant-Tail Floating Nymph on the left has a parachute hackle; the fly on the right is a no-hackle version. Use the nymph with the parachute hackle when casting to rising trout during a hatch. The no-hackle model is used when dead-drift nymphing during the earliest stage of an emergence when the trout are still feeding well below the surface.

rising to duns. As it turned out, the stomach samples contained more emerging nymphs than duns. They recommended fishing the Floating Nymph as a dry fly to rising trout.

Since Swisher and Richards introduced their Floating Nymph in the late 1970s, the design has undergone several variations. Fred Arbona Jr. described one version in his book *Mayflies, the Angler and the Trout*. This fly is tied with a hackle-barb tail, a large dubbing ball, and a few hackle fibers tied in as legs to aid flotation. Arbona said the fly is particularly effective for simulating the nymphs of smaller mayfly species struggling at the surface to escape their shucks. Gary Borger popularized another variation of the Floating Nymph by winding a parachute hackle around the base of the dubbing ball to give the fly even better flotation. The Parachute Floating Nymph remains the most popular variation of the Swisher-Richards idea.

I tie both parachute and no-hackle floating nymphs. I use the Parachute Floating Nymph when fishing to rising trout because of its superior buoyancy. It's also easier to see on the water's surface. I use the No-Hackle Floating Nymph at the beginning of the hatch before the topwater action starts. I like to place a bit of weight twelve to twenty inches above the fly. The buoyant polypropylene dubbing ball causes the no-hackle

imitation to rise in the water just like an emerging nymph on its way to the surface. It's deadly before the hatch. A hackled version would be just as effective, but I find it difficult to waste good hackle on a fly that I intend to fish as a nymph.

Trailing the Parachute or No-Hackle Floating Nymph behind a dry fly is a popular way to fish these patterns. Simply tie a twelve- to eighteen-inch piece of tippet material to the bend of a dry-fly hook with a clinch knot, and tie a floating nymph to the end of the tippet. The dry fly acts as a strike indicator if a fish takes the nymph. This system allows you to appeal to the trout taking duns as well as those feeding on emergers.

Floating nymphs work well for most hatches of small mayflies. When the pale morning duns come off on western tailwaters and spring creeks, it takes them a long time to get out of their shucks and into the air. This situation begs for the Pheasant-Tail Floating Nymph. I tie this fly in sizes 16 to 22 with a brown hackle-barb tail, a copper-wire rib, a pheasant-tail abdomen, a ball of Fly-Rite ginger cream polypropylene dubbing or a similar ginger-colored synthetic dubbing (the ginger color is important!), and a brown hackle wrapped parachute style. The Pheasant-Tail Floating Nymph also holds its own during blue-winged olive hatches.

PHEASANT-TAIL FLOATING NYMPH

Hook:	Standard dry-fly hook, sizes 16 to 20.
Thread:	Brown 8/0 to 14/0.
Tail:	Brown hackle barbs.
Body:	Pheasant-tail fibers.
Thorax:	Brown Umpqua Superfine or a similar dubbing.
Rib:	Fine copper wire.
Dubbing ball:	Fine ginger or tannish cream polypropylene dubbing.
Hackle:	Brown, one size smaller than normal.

Step 1. Start the thread. Tie on several hackle barbs for the tail. Attach a piece of copper wire.

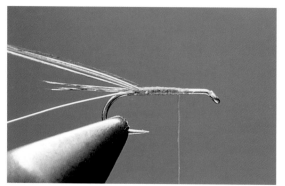

Step 2. Tie on the tips of several pheasant-tail fibers.

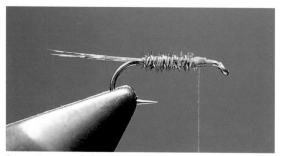

Step 3. Wind the pheasant-tail fibers forward to form the body. Tie them off and clip the excess. Wrap the wire up the body to form the rib.

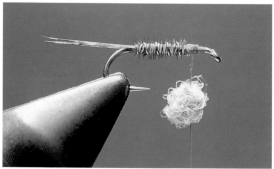

Step 4. Apply a narrow strand of polypropylene dubbing to the thread and form a dubbing ball.

Step 5. Position the tying thread and the dubbing ball directly above the hook shank.

Step 6. Slide the dubbing ball down to the hook shank and secure it with a few wraps of thread in front of it and behind it and then a few wraps of thread around the base. Attach the hackle shiny side up.

Step 1. Attach the trailing-shuck material at the bend of the hook.

Step 2. Tie in a strand of sparkle yarn across the hook with crisscross wraps.

Step 3. Dub the body, leaving a little room behind the hook eye.

Step 4. Tease out the sparkle yarn with a dubbing needle.

Step 5. Pull the sparkle yarn over the top, forming a hump. The hump is easier to form if you pull the yarn up a bit with a dubbing needle.

Step 6. Tie down the sparkle yarn and tie off the thread. Trim the yarn, leaving a short stub.

Imitations of adult microcaddis can be as simple as dubbed bodies and wings of elk hair (left) or CDC fibers (right). Pulling these flies below the surface at the end of the drift will often trigger a strike, suggesting that the trout take them as female caddis diving to lay their eggs.

ADULT MICROCADDIS IMITATIONS

I also experimented with a few adult caddisfly imitations. One is a simple, small-fly version of the Elk Hair Caddis on which the hackle is deleted. To help the fly stay on top, I flared the elk hair a little more on the sides of the wing and then greased it. On hooks size 18 and smaller, the elk hair alone is enough to float the fly in the surface film. Although I occasionally picked up trout on this fly during the hatch, its effectiveness was a hit-or-miss proposition. What I learned, however, was that it was more effective when pulled under the surface at the end of the drift and on the swing.

Another option is a parachute caddisfly pattern. On this parachute caddisfly, the hackle is tied *above* the wing rather than below it. Putting the hackle above the wing pushes the wing down into the surface film. The body of the fly is actually on the *underside* of the surface film. If you've ever looked at crippled or stillborn mayfly duns, midges, or caddisflies, you've noticed that this is the way they lie on the water. In addition to microcaddis, I've used various renditions of this pattern for midge hatches and blue-winged olive hatches. For want of a better name I call it the All-Around because I've used it successfully for so many different small-fly hatches.

THE ALL-AROUND

Hook:	Any down-eye dry-fly hook size 18 or smaller.
Thread:	8/0 to 14/0; color to match wing material.
Abdomen and thorax:	Very fine-textured dubbing; color to match the natural.
Hackle:	Barred ginger, grizzly, or cree.
Wing:	Bleached elk or deer hair; Z-Lon for very small flies.

Step 2. Tie in a small bunch of elk hair. Bend up the butt ends of the hair to form a post. Make several wraps of thread at the base of the post.

Step 1. Tie on the thread and wrap back to the bend. Dub the abdomen.

Step 3. Tie in the hackle at the base of the post.

Step 4. Wrap the hackle around the post. Secure the hackle with your thread, and clip the tip of the feather.

Step 5. Tie off the thread with a whip-finish or half-hitches. Trim the post down to just above the hackle.

Step 6. Place a drop of Zap-A-Gap on the post.

This pattern is adaptable, so don't be afraid to experiment. For general-purpose microcaddis imitations, I like bleached elk hock for the wing in hook sizes down to 22. Look for hair that still has some brown highlights, rather than hair that is completely bleached out. For specific hatches, like the black microcaddis, I match wing color to the natural. For hook sizes smaller than 22 I often switch to Z-Lon for the wing to avoid bulk.

I'm a big fan of barred hackle for caddisfly patterns because it gives the impression of movement—like the fluttering wings of the struggling natural in the surface film. I use fine synthetic dubbing, such as Umpqua's Superfine, for very small microcaddis imitations, but for size 20 and larger flies I often use a dubbing blend that includes some spiky material.

The parachute hackle is wrapped around a post formed from the wing material. Wrap the tying thread far enough up the bottom of the post to form a base for the hackle. Strip the barbs from the base of the hackle feather and tie it in with the concave side at the base of the wing post. Then bind the stem to the wing-post base and wrap it down from the top. The hackle is then tied off either at the base of the post or at the head. Once the hackle is secured, cut away the wing material above the base of the post. The fly is finished with a drop of Zap-A-Gap on top of the now-stubby post to increase the durability of the hackle and firm up the post. For small flies, it pays to make a finer bodkin out of a No. 12 beading needle for applying the Zap-A-Gap.

Patterns tied with cul-de-canard (CDC) also proved useful. Initially, I just tied a tuft of the material in a downwing position over the hook shank. Then I learned to make a higher-floating version by tying small bundles of CDC barbs from the bend of the hook all the way to the eye, and then trimming them to the tent-like shape of a caddisfly's wings. My CDC patterns worked very well during hatches of small caddisflies other than the black microcaddis, but they garnered only the occasional strike during the black microcaddis hatch. Like my elk-hair flies, the CDC patterns were most effective when pulled under, either at the end of the drift or on the swing.

BUNDLED CDC MICROCADDIS

Hook: TMC 100 or 101, sizes 18 to 22.

Thread: 8/0 to 14/0 to match body of the natural.

Body: The tying thread.

Wing: Bundles of CDC barbs bound to the hook and trimmed to shape.

Note: This is a miniature version of a western caddisfly pattern that utilizes bundles of deer hair tied on the top of the entire length of the hook shank. That's not practical on small hooks, but CDC is. Simply tie the bundles of CDC barbs to the top of the hook and then trim them to the shape of a caddisfly. It floats like a cork. In *Micropatterns,* Darrel Martin describes a similar fly, the Riffle Sedge, tied by Taff Price.

Step 1. Wind the tying thread to the rear of the hook. Tie a small bundle of CDC barbs atop the shank. Advance the thread a little and tie in another bundle. Continue the process up the hook shank.

Step 2. Once all the bundles have been mounted, form a head and whip-finish.

Step 3. If necessary, trim or pluck the CDC to the form of a caddisfly.

DIVING FEMALE CADDIS

I picked away at the black microcaddis mystery until the day I decided to call Gary LaFontaine. He picked right up on the caddis crawling up my waders.

"What you probably have there are diving females that are swimming below the surface to lay their eggs," he said, while being very careful to state that he couldn't make a "definitive" judgment unless I sent him a few bugs to look at. But that alone explained why my adult elk-hair and CDC caddisfly imitations were working better when pulled under the surface than when fished on top.

Gary suggested that I tie some diving caddis imitations, which I'd have figured out on my own if I'd just read his book more carefully. He recommended fishing them in a gang of three with a yarn strike indicator. The idea was to mend a little slack into the drift so the flies wouldn't swing too severely and would present broadside to the trout. He said that the imitations should be tied with bodies to match the naturals, using the clear Antron overwing that he described in his book.

After talking with Gary, I sat down at the vise and began tying size 20 LaFontaine Diving Caddis imitations with black bodies, dark grouse-fiber underwings, clear Antron overwings, and sparse, dark blue-dun hackles. The next time I was on the river, the ganged Diving Caddis imitations did indeed work better than any of my other attempts to match the microcaddis hatch. The trout still didn't hit the flies on every cast, but the strikes were consistent enough that I was never bored. They took the ganged flies both on the mend and on the swing. I was a happy camper.

LAFONTAINE DIVING CADDIS

Hook: TMC 100, size 18 or 20.
Thread: 8/0, color to match body.
Body: Hare's-ear or Antron dubbing in a color
              to match the natural.
Underwing: Grouse or partridge fibers. For an imita-
              tion of the black microcaddis, use fibers
              from a dark feather.
Overwing: Clear Antron.
Hackle: Dun.

Step 2. Tie in the underwing.

Step 1. Dub a thin body, leaving some room at the front.

Step 3. Attach the Antron overwing.

Step 4. Add one or two wraps of hackle and finish the head.

I still have a lot to learn about microcaddis, but I do know that if they're found in sufficient numbers, the trout will not neglect them. Since I'm still learning, I haven't really codified what I carry to cover the stages of microcaddis, but right now my box contains the Larva Lace imitation, a few dubbed larva imitations, the Brassie to imitate other small case-building caddis larvae, bead-head Emergent Sparkle Pupa patterns for fishing deep, unweighted Emergent Sparkle Pupa to be fished on the surface and in middle depths, the Micro Devil Bug, LaFontaine's Diving Caddis, the hackleless Elk Hair Caddis, and the CDC adult microcaddis imitations.

The trout in my area seem especially fond of light tan sparkle-yarn overbodies and trailing shucks with a hint of orange in them. I tie dark Antron or hare's-ear bodies for darker species and olive, light brown, or rusty orange for lighter-colored caddisflies. The trout in your area may have different tastes. If I had to pick one single pattern for the bulging and porpoising trout, it would be the Micro Devil Bug, followed closely by the LaFontaine Diving Caddis.

That's what I know now. There's still a lot to learn, and I'm working on it. More than anything, that's what rings my chimes with fly fishing. You can learn all the time.

And you should know that I don't fear the dreaded black microcaddis hatch quite as much as I used to.

CHAPTER FOURTEEN

Microscuds

It has been my privilege to teach many fly-fishing classes over the years. My students and I always seine the river as a part of the course. The idea is to collect a sample of aquatic trout foods, identify them, and then show the students how to select flies that match the naturals.

The river where I've done most of my teaching always produces a healthy sample of scuds. A scud, sometimes mistakenly referred to as freshwater shrimp, is a laterally flattened crustacean with the head and first thoracic segment fused together to form the cephalothorax. A scud has seven pairs of legs, the first two modified for grasping. Most scuds live in shallow-water aquatic vegetation.

Scuds are highly proficient swimmers and can be quite prolific in the cold, alkaline, highly oxygenated water associated with tailwaters, spring creeks, and stillwaters. They are one of the power foods contributing to the high growth rates of trout in these environments.

The samples of scuds seined by my classes have always contained specimens of several sizes. I always assumed that the smaller scuds must be immature forms of the larger ones. My view changed one day when I realized that a typical sample actually contained mostly small and large scuds with few of the in-between sizes. The new information caused me to alter my reasoning a bit. I began to think that the small scuds must simply be a new brood that would grow to "normal" size.

My comfortable logic was shattered later that season when it occurred to me that the small scuds were *always* the same size and that the larger scuds, which did vary a bit in size, were always larger than the small scuds. There were never enough in-between sizes! Logically, it seemed that if the small scuds were indeed new broods, then sooner or later I should see a majority of in-between sizes or at least a reduction in the quite numerous small scuds. But there were always lots of little scuds. It was time to figure out what was really going on.

I hit the books and quickly learned that many trout waters contain two common scuds. One species is large and the other is small. The larger scuds come from the family Gammaridae. The most common genus is *Gammarus,* the members of which usually run from about size 14 to 18. These are the scuds you most often read about in the fly-fishing literature.

The smaller species is the widely distributed *Hyalella azteca*. It runs from about size 18 to 24. These microscuds are quite prolific and are an important food source for trout. The year-round existence of a small scud explains why the smaller scud imitations that have become so popular on western tailwaters work so well. It just hadn't occurred to me that these patterns were actually imitating a scud species that never grows up.

IDEAS FOR TYING SMALL SCUDS

My research turned up some other interesting facts about scuds. Depending on which authority you read, many species of scuds breed only once in their lives (*Naturals* by Gary Borger), whereas others are profoundly fertile (*Nymphs*, by Ernest Schwiebert). More important is whether the scud should be tied on a curved hook, which represents the curled-up defensive position it assumes when seined from the water, or on a straight hook in the stretched-out position that it actually swims in. If you are a match-the-hatch sort of person, you'll want the straight-hook imitation because these are how the real scuds typically appear to trout. I'm more of a let's-try-it-and-see kind of person and have tied scud imitations on both curved and straight hooks. I can't say the fish prefer one over the other. That's why there is a sample of each type in this chapter.

After discovering that microscuds live in many of the western waters I fish, my first move was simply to reduce the size of my standard shellback scud imitation. The almost universal shellback-style scud pattern is tied with a dubbed body, a thin strip of plastic pulled over the top to imitate the back, and a rib of thin wire or monofilament. Some shellback scud imitations include hackle-fiber tails and even antennae at the head, but these features aren't absolutely crucial. The dubbing is picked out on the bottom of the fly to represent legs as the final step.

SHELLBACK MICROSCUD

Hook:	TMC 2487, TMC 2488, or equivalent curved hook, sizes 18 to 22.
Thread:	8/0 to 14/0 in a color to match the natural.
Tail (optional):	Hackle barbs in a color to match the natural.
Rib:	Fine gold or copper wire or 5X monofilament.
Shellback:	Plastic from a Ziploc bag or pearlescent Mylar.
Body:	Rabbit fur, rabbit fur/synthetic mix, Hareline Krystal Dub.

Step 1. Tie in the monofilament rib and the plastic shellback. The plastic shellback should be cut wide enough to cover the top of the finished fly, but not go down too far over the sides.

Step 2. Dub a stout, tapered body.

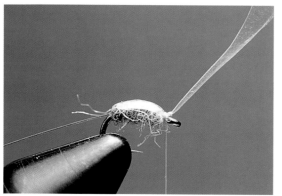

Step 3. Pull the plastic shellback over the top of the fly and tie it down behind the hook eye. Trim the excess plastic strip.

Step 4. Wind the monofilament rib and tie it off behind the hook eye. Trim the excess monofilament. Form a head and whip-finish.

Step 5. Use a needle to pick out dubbing from the bottom of the fly. This will create the illusion of legs.

Step 6. The legs should be slightly longer toward the front of the finished fly.

You can substitute pearlescent Mylar for the plastic back to create a flashier scud. I typically use plain rabbit fur or rabbit fur mixed with a flashy synthetic dubbing for the body, but I occasionally mix a pure synthetic dubbing to create an even brighter body. My standard colors are tan, gray, and olive.

I also tie an orange scud. The party line behind this color is that scuds turn orange when they die, at which point they are readily available to trout. Other theories reckon that the scuds are orange when molting or filled with eggs. As sweet as this logic sounds, it's just as easy for me to believe that orange scud flies are great egg imitations. They seem most effective in my area when the water is up in the spring and the rainbow trout are on the spawn. I know fly fishers who would never consider fishing an egg pattern but adore the orange scud! Whatever *you* think, orange is just a naturally fishy color and there is no question that orange scud imitations catch trout.

A standard shellback scud can be reduced to smaller sizes by simply cutting the plastic strip for the back a little narrower. Flashier Mylar is also available in widths appropriate for tying small scuds.

It's important to carry some weighted scud patterns for those times when the trout are working the shallow-water aquatic vegetation. These patterns can be fished directly to the trout without the usual dead-drift nymphing paraphernalia such as split shot and strike indicators. Some tiers lightly weight their larger scud imitations by adding wraps of lead wire around the hook shank. Although this is possible for smaller patterns with thinner lead wire, many tiers simply tie the pattern unweighted and rely on weight added to the leader to sink the fly. An alternative is to lash a section of large-diameter wire to the top of the shank. In addition to adding weight to the fly, this wire can be flattened with pliers to help create the flat silhouette of the natural.

Another useful microscud imitation was popularized by South Platte River fly fisher Roger Hill. The pattern is nothing more than a dubbed body trimmed into the laterally compressed shape of a scud. A chenille of synthetic or rabbit-fur dubbing is made with a dubbing loop and wrapped around the shank and tied off. The sides and top are then trimmed to form the shape of the scud. The fly is completed by winding the wire rib forward and picking out any dubbing fibers that may have been trapped under it.

HILL'S SCUD

Hook:	TMC 2487 or TMC 2488, sizes 18 to 22.	Note:	Use a dubbing loop to make a chenille. Wrap the chenille forward over the shank. Trim the top and sides of the body to shape the scud imitation.
Thread:	8/0 to 14/0 in a color to match the natural.		
Rib:	Fine copper wire.		
Body:	Rabbit fur or equivalent, flashy synthetic dubbing, or a mix of the two.		

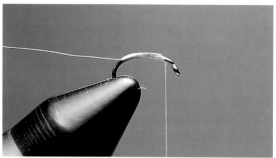

Step 1. Tie the rib to the shank. Wrap the thread well down into the hook bend.

Step 2. Form a dubbing loop with the thread, fill it with dubbing material, and twist it into a chenille.

Step 3. Wrap the chenille forward. Smooth the fibers toward the rear after each turn. Tie the chenille off.

Step 4. Trim the sides and top of the fly very close to the hook shank.

Step 5. Wind the rib forward. Tie off. Pick out any fibers that got trapped under the rib.

A more obscure pattern came to my attention a number of years ago in Montana. Although originated to imitate larger scuds, the pattern reduces nicely to smaller sizes and is especially effective in slow or still water. Adding weight with fuse wire lashed to the hook shank is optional for moving waters, but necessary if the fly is to be used in still water. A tail of medium-dun hackle barbs is also an option.

First, tie in a fine gold wire or monofilament rib near the hook bend. Then attach a section of a secondary mallard quill for the shellback and an aftershaft feather found at the base of a partridge feather. Next, tie in two strands of gray ostrich herl. Twist the ostrich herl around the tying thread, wrap it forward, and tie it off at the head. At this point, pull the aftershaft feather over the back, followed by the mallard shellback. Rib the fly with the gold wire and tie off. It may be necessary to trim the ostrich herl to hook-gap length.

ALL-NATURAL MICROSCUD

Hook: TMC 100, sizes 18 to 22.
Thread: Gray 8/0 to 10/0.
Rib: Fine gold wire.
Tail: Blue-dun hackle barbs.
Body: Gray ostrich herl.
Shellback: A few sections of a gray mallard primary or secondary wing quill and a partridge aftershaft feather.

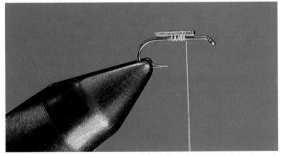

Step 1. Tie a piece of lead wire to the hook shank.

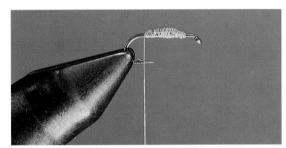

Step 2. Flatten the ends of the lead wire with pliers and cover it evenly with thread.

Step 3. Tie on some hackle fibers to create a short tail. Tie on a piece of wire for making the rib.

Step 4. Select an aftershaft feather from the base of a partridge body feather.

Step 7. Wrap the thread and ostrich herl up the hook to form the body. Tie off and clip the excess herl.

Step 5. Tie in a section of mallard feather at the base of the tail. Tie in the partridge aftershaft feather flat on top of the mallard.

Step 8. Pull the aftershaft feather over the top of the fly, tie it off, and clip the excess.

Step 6. Tie in two strands of ostrich herl. Twist the herl around the thread.

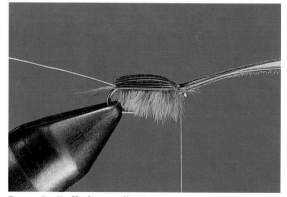

Step 9. Pull the mallard section over the top to form the shellback and tie it off.

Step 10. Clip the excess mallard. Wind the rib, tie it off, and clip the excess wire. Make a neat thread head.

I picked up the final pattern in Arkansas when its originator, Brooks Handly, gave me a few to try on the North Fork of the White River. It worked quite well, and when I tried it back home in Colorado, the trout couldn't get enough of this unique pattern. I later asked Brooks if he'd mind if I wrote about the Humpback Scud.

"Of course you can show my scud, but are you sure you want to turn that pattern loose on the country's fish population?" he joked. "I'm sure there will be a couple of my buddies that won't like it, but they'll get over it. They think we have the secret weapon even though I try to assure them there are no secrets left in fly fishing."

Tie the Humpback Scud on a Tiemco TMC 205BL hook, size 20. The shape of the hook is the basis of forming a realistic scud profile. The key to the fly is a piece of Twiston lead (a flat lead tape used by nymphers to add weight to leaders) trimmed into an elongated half-moon shape and lashed to the top of the hook to weight the fly. Once the weight is in place, tie in a piece of Hareline Scud Back, a very flexible latex-like material, at the bend of the hook, along with a piece of 5X monofilament for a rib. Dub rabbit fur (I prefer straight rabbit fur or Hareline Dubbin's Krystal Dub if I want a bit more flash) in a color to match the natural tightly onto the thread and wrap it forward in evenly spaced segments. Pull the Scud Back over the top of the fly and finish by winding the rib forward between the segments.

HANDLY HUMPBACK SCUD

Hook: TMC 205BL, size 20.

Thread: 8/0 in a color to the match the natural.

Hump: Twiston lead trimmed to shape.

Rib: 5X monofilament.

Body: Rabbit fur in a color to match the natural.

Shellback: A strip of one-eighth-inch Hareline Scud Back in a color to match the natural.

Note: The "Hump" is made by pre-cutting small triangles from Twiston lead. Dead-drift nymph fishermen use Twiston lead to add weight to leader. Look for this product in your local fly shop.

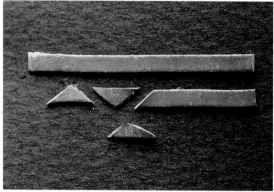

Step 1. Prepare a strip of Twiston lead (top) by cutting it into a series of triangles (middle). Trim the "point" at the top of the triangle.

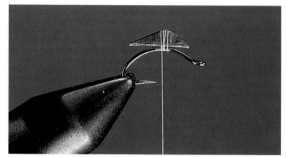

Step 2. Lash the Twiston triangle to the top of the hook, beginning in the middle of the lead.

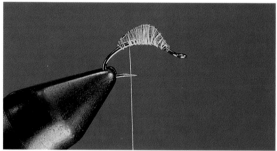

Step 3. When the middle of the lead is tightly secured to the hook, bend the ends down to form a hump-like shape. Wind the thread out from the middle of the lead. Secure the lead with thread wraps.

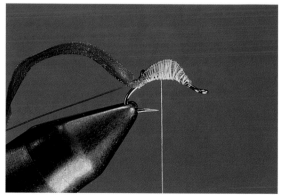

Step 4. Tie in the monofilament and the Hareline Scud Back at the end of the hook.

Step 5. Apply the dubbing tightly to the thread and wrap the body, creating a rib-like effect.

Step 6. Pull the Scud Back over the top of the fly, forming a shellback. Tie it in at the hook eye and clip the excess material.

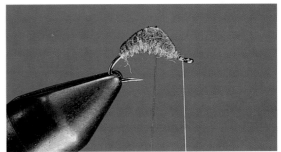

Step 7. Wind the rib forward in between the wraps of dubbing material.

The result is a highly effective, fast-sinking scud pattern for dead-drift nymphing, sight-fishing to trout you find working the weeds, and casting to cruising fish.

Microscud imitations work. They have proved especially productive for me on the hard-fished Front Range tailwaters in Colorado. The next time you fish waters inhabited by these tiny crustaceans, give microscuds a try.

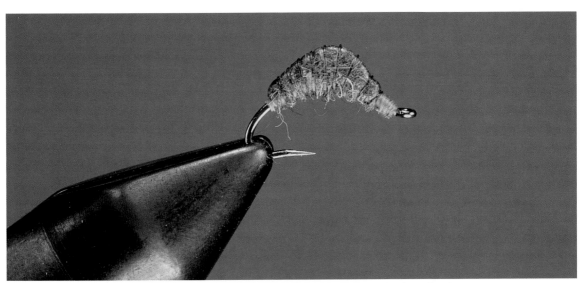

Step 8. Tie down the rib material at the hook eye, form a head, and whip-finish.

CHAPTER FIFTEEN

Tiny Ants

A number of years ago I traveled from my home in Colorado to Pennsylvania. The plan was to take the southeastern Pennsylvania limestone spring creeks by storm. At the time, I'd fallen into the trap of thinking I was a "young gun," a term some folks were applying to a breed of hot, young fishing guides that specialized in the use of small flies on Colorado's fabled tailwaters.

My claim to young-gun status came from more than a decade of fly-fishing experience on Colorado's South Platte River. I'd developed a fair level of mastery over the river's tricky blue-winged olive, pale morning dun, and microcaddis hatches. I'd also come a long way in figuring out the sometimes maddeningly difficult midge hatches on the river. It turned out that with a little tinkering, the small-fly patterns and tactics that worked on the South Platte worked well on the other blue-ribbon western tailwaters such as San Juan River, Dolores River, Blue River, Green River, and Taylor River. The patterns and tactics also stood up well on western spring creeks.

Along the way I'd also managed to become a successful guide on the South Platte and San Juan. All told, the situation had me thinking I was pretty competent.

That's the state of mind I was in when I stepped off the airplane in Washington, D.C., and headed north to the legendary spring creeks of southeastern Pennsylvania.

When I found myself standing waist deep in a long, flat, tree-lined stretch of the Yellow Breeches with trout dimpling around me, I knew exactly what to do. The trout were clearly rising to emerging midges. I saw no bubbles in the rise-forms, but I could see the fish leisurely working just under the surface. I tied on a favorite midge-emerger pattern and laid out a cast. The results were negative. I made more casts. And the results remained negative. I changed flies. I lengthened tippets. I tried different casts. . . .

An hour later the trout were still dimpling sporadically and I still hadn't had a strike. Finally, I waded downstream, got out my seine, and took a sample of the drift. When I lifted the seine from the water I noticed a number of tiny, size 22, cinnamon-colored ants. Naturally, I didn't have anything close to a match in my fly box. I retired to the fly-tying vise. I also got to thinking that maybe I was a little too old to be calling myself a young gun.

Almost any southeastern Pennsylvania fly fisher could have told me what was going on at the

Yellow Breeches that day. Pennsylvanians are masters of terrestrial and small-fly fishing. As I spent more time in Pennsylvania, I came to learn that terrestrials play a very important part in the angling there. The tree-lined banks of the Yellow Breeches should have told me that the *odds* of more terrestrials falling into the water were greater there than on the western rivers I call home.

Eastern anglers are simply more aware than their Rocky Mountain counterparts of the potential of catching trout on terrestrial patterns. I brought my newfound knowledge back to Colorado and found to my surprise that tiny ant patterns work very well on our western tailwaters. It's just that western anglers never think to use them. It may be that they are too wrapped up in dead-drift nymphing tactics to realize the power of the tiny ant.

Since my trip to Pennsylvania I've had many delightful afternoons on the South Platte using tiny ant patterns to search the banks for larger-than-average trout. It's a wonderful way to break up the monotony of endless hours of dead-drift nymphing. It has allowed me to take the strike indicators and lead off the leader and cast the fly rod the way it was meant to be cast—and pick up some fish.

As a rule, ants end up on the water's surface in two ways. Wingless ants tend to appear randomly when they fall into the water. Usually it's just a sporadic thing, but on occasion you find them in higher numbers. That's the way it was on the Yellow Breeches, though I don't know why. More typically, you'll find a lot of ants on the surface when a swarm of the winged variety has been blown onto the water. Most anglers are clued to the winged-ant phenomenon because it's as good as manna. The trout go nuts.

What some anglers haven't learned is that many species of ants are quite small. While it's easy to pick up on larger ants, trout rising to smaller ants can be mistaken for fish rising to midges. It pays to check the water. It also pays to remember that trout just like eating ants. Even when there are no ants on the water, a small ant imitation can pull fish up when used as a searching pattern along the banks.

THE LACQUERED-THREAD ANT

I've carried a variety of ant patterns over the years. Most small patterns are simply scaled-down versions of larger imitations. Like many western anglers, I started with a simple lacquered-thread pattern that I picked up from Jack Dennis's *Western Trout Fly Tying Manual.*

LACQUERED-THREAD ANT

Hook:	Dry-fly hook, turned-down eye, sizes 18 to 24.	Hackle:	To match the color of the natural.
Thread:	6/0 or 8/0, in a color to match the natural.	Tag (optional):	Red thread or floss.
Gaster:	Built up with thread.	Note:	Lacquer the body sections when complete, or use glossy black enamel paint for added luster.
Head:	Built up with thread.		

Lacquered-thread ant. You can fish this traditional pattern as a dry fly or beneath the surface as a wet fly. This fly has a tag of red thread.

The pattern is tied by simply building up the rear abdomen, or, more correctly, the gaster, of the ant with thread. A thin spot is left to represent where the abdomen is pinched into a characteristic narrow waist, called the pedicel, and then another, slightly less enlarged "bump" of thread is tied to represent the head of the ant. A more exacting imitation would actually represent three distinct sections, but most anglers find the "two-bumped" version gets the job done. To finish the fly, a few winds of hackle are added in the narrow section to represent legs. On all traditionally hackled ant patterns I make the hackle hook-gap length. In Dennis's version there is a tag of red thread or floss. The gaster and head are then lacquered, but a coating of Testor's enamel paint works just as well. The lacquered-thread ant is typically tied in black, but brown, red, or cinnamon-colored thread may be used to cover brown or red ant species.

The traditional lacquered-thread ant imitation has several advantages. First, it tends to sink into the surface film. This is important because both winged and wingless ants sink into the film. The lacquered-thread version can also be fished wet, an effective presentation for an ant pattern that many fly fishers overlook. When I first started tying lacquered-thread ants, the quality of dry-fly hackle was not nearly what it is today, which was actually an advantage: It helped the fly sink into the film. Today's high-quality genetic hackle may actually float the fly too high. A simple solution is to trim the bottom half of the hackle.

TINY DUBBED ANT IMITATIONS

Dubbed ant imitations have become increasingly popular. The design is the same as that of a thread ant: an enlarged gaster and somewhat smaller head. Although the body sections can be dubbed and wound around the hook shank, many tiers now use the dubbing-ball technique developed by René Harrop. A small ball of dubbing is formed on the tying thread and then slid down *on top* of the hook shank to form each body section. This approach allows the fly to sit down in the film, and doesn't encroach on the gap of a tiny hook. Once again, a hackle is wound around the narrow pedicel. A low-lying option for dubbed ants uses a parachute hackle wound around the base of the forward ball of dubbing.

A WINGLESS, DUBBED PARACHUTE ANT

Hook:	Dry-fly hook, turned-down eye, sizes 18 to 22.
Thread:	8/0 to 14/0 in a color to match the natural.
Body:	Fine ball of dubbing in a color to match the natural.
Hackle:	Color to match the natural.

Step 2. Slide the dubbing ball down the thread and onto the top of the hook to form the gaster. Spin another dubbing ball on the thread and slide it down to the hook to form the head.

Step 1. Start the thread on the hook and wrap to the bend. Spin a ball of dubbing on the thread.

Step 3. Tie a hackle in at the base of the head.

Step 4. Wrap the hackle under the dubbed head of the fly. Tie off the feather and whip-finish the thread.

Every fly box should contain a few bright ants. These flies do a good job of imitating red and cinnamon-colored ants. The specimen on the left has a dubbed body and head; the one on the right is made of large-cell foam colored with a marker.

For tiny ant imitations, I prefer very fine synthetic dubbing such as Umpqua's Superfine or Sparkle Blend. If you prefer natural materials, beaver makes a nice ant. Dubbing offers a wide range of color options. I carry traditional black and brown or cinnamon imitations, plus a few very bright red or orange imitations. The "bright" ants have saved me on any number of occasions, both when the trout were rising to ants and even during difficult midge hatches when nothing else worked.

FOAM ANTS

The most recent trend in ant patterns has been the use of various foams. Dense, colored foam (Polycelon) is cut into a thin strip and bound down near the center of the hook shank to form the pedicel. The foam extending from the rear of the hook is folded over to form the gaster and is then bound down at the pedicel. The foam extending over the front of the hook is folded back and tied down at the pedicel to form the head. Once again, a few wraps of hackle around the pedicel form legs. The bottom half of the hackle may be trimmed to allow the fly to sit down in the surface film.

DENSE FOAM (POLYCELON) ANTS

Hook: Dry-fly hook, turned-down eye, sizes 18 to 22.
Thread: 8/0 to 14/0 in a color to match the natural.
Body: Dense folded foam.
Hackle: Color to match the natural.

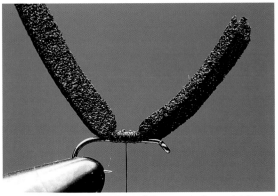

Step 1. Tie in a strip of foam at the middle of the hook shank.

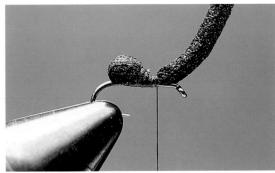

Step 2. Fold over the foam at the rear of the fly and tie it off to form the gaster.

Step 3. Fold over the foam at the front of the fly to form the head. The head should be slightly smaller than the gaster.

Step 4. Attach and wrap a hackle at the ant's waist.

Real ants float low in the surface film; imitations should do likewise. Clip the hackle on the bottom of an ant so the fly rests properly on the water.

Gary LaFontaine pioneered the use of large-cell polyurethane foam for ant imitations. The translucent material is colored with waterproof marking pens to match the naturals. These patterns have been quite effective for me on my home waters, though they don't hold up quite as well as imitations tied with denser foam. The patterns are tied the same way as those utilizing the more dense foams: tie in a strip of material near the center of the hook and fold each end back toward the pedicel to form the gaster and head. A few wraps of hackle are then wound over the pedicel.

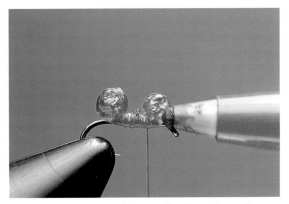

Gary LaFontaine used large-cell polyurethane foam to make ant imitations. The foam is tied to the hook in the same way that a dense foam ant is made. LaFontaine colored the clear foam with waterproof marking pens.

When the foam has been colored, a hackle is added at the pedicel (waist).

WINGED ANTS

Winged versions of all of the non-winged patterns are easy to produce. For down-wing patterns, simply tie in Antron, straight Z-Lon, or a similar material at the narrow pedicel. The wing should lie back over the gaster and extend somewhat beyond the bend of the hook. I usually add a few turns of hackle at the pedicel to complete the fly, but that's optional. Some tiers use a more rigid material such as Medallion Sheeting or Zing to form the wing. Either of these creates a more sheet-like effect and lies flat over the gaster.

A final wing option that should be considered is the upright wing. I've found that in some cases an upright wing is more effective than the down wing, though perhaps I'm splitting hairs.

Nonetheless, I do carry a few upright-wing versions of several ant patterns. If nothing else, they are easier to see on the water's surface if light conditions are difficult.

An effective upright-wing ant variation utilizes a post of polypropylene or similar material. In *Designing Trout Flies,* Gary Borger makes a nifty rendition by tying in the post just behind the hook eye. He forms a dubbing ball around the base of the post and winds a few turns of hackle parachute style around the bottom of the dubbing ball. The result is a fine low-riding imitation. Other tiers simply tie in dun-colored hackle-tip wings at the pedicel and make a few wraps of hackle on either side. Hackle-tip wings may also be tied in a spent position.

Winged ants can be tied with or without hackle. No-hackle ants sit lower on the water and may be more effective.

Upright, hackle-tip wings are easy to see in poor light or on broken water.

WINGED PARACHUTE ANT

Hook: Dry-fly hook, turned-down eye, sizes 18 to 22.

Thread: 8/0 to 14/0 in a color to match the natural.

Body: Fine ball of dubbing to match the color of the natural.

Hackle: Color to match the natural.

Wing: Krystal Flash, Antron, poly yarn, or a similar material.

Step 1. Dub the gaster. Fold the wing material under the front half of the hook shank.

Step 2. Secure the wing material with a criss-cross wrap.

Step 4. Wrap a base of thread at the bottom of the wing. Spin a little dubbing on the thread.

Step 3. Tie on a hackle at the base of the wing.

Step 5. Wrap the dubbed thread around the wing post to form the head of the ant.

Step 6. Wrap the hackle under the dubbed head. Tie off the feather and whip-finish the thread. Cut the wing to length.

One final ant pattern is a simple modification of the always effective Griffith's Gnat. Simply form a gaster and head of peacock herl and hackle it at the pedicel with grizzly. It's another one of those patterns that can save the day in a pinch.

Although it isn't necessary to devote an entire fly box to myriad ant imitations, I reserve a corner of my dry-fly box for several variations of both winged and wingless versions. I always carry black, cinnamon, and red or orange ants. Until recently, they spent most of the time sitting in reserve for those days when I actually found ants on the water or those rare, glorious days when winged ants were in the air.

Lately, I find myself turning to the tiny ants more and more when things slow down toward midday and early afternoon. I like to work them along the grassy banks of the South Platte River, dropping casts in front of and behind little tufts of grass and other obstructions that jut into the river. I pass them over the deeper slots and next to undercut banks. I cast them into the grass and pull them on to the water's surface. I drown them and fish them wet.

And I wait for the dimple of recognition from one of the big boys taking it easy near the bank, exactly where most anglers don't look for trout when the sun is high overhead.

The Peacock Ant is a modification of the Griffith's Gnat.

CHAPTER SIXTEEN

Tiny, Simple, Old, New, and Effective Small-Fly Patterns

A number of years ago I got into a serious jag of midge fishing on the San Juan River below Navajo Dam in northwestern New Mexico. At the time, the angling technique of choice on the San Juan was dead-drift nymph fishing, but a group of us met on the river nearly every day to work the difficult, smutting trout that could be found in backwater sloughs and quiet channels.

A standard day of San Juan midging for me back then typically consisted of taking one or two trout and casting a variety of patterns. I never seemed to find a "silver bullet" fly that took fish consistently, but I was happy enough. We all knew the fishing could be tough. I had one pal, a real fly-tying machine, who came to the river armed each day with dozens of "new" patterns to try out. Once in a while he hit the mark, too.

I remember one afternoon when he was enjoying a good measure of success. We both had observed that the trout were rising regularly to adult midges. If you fish midges much, you know that this is not an altogether common occurrence; most often the trout are on the pupae. But on that day we could actually see the fish taking winged adults off the surface. The midges were in the process of mating and you could see a few skating over the water's surface while others formed swarms. A light breeze occasionally blew a cluster of them along the surface.

When I asked my pal what he was using, he proudly showed me his "Knotted Midge" pattern. It was tied to imitate two midges firmly joined in the act. I examined it closely. The simple fly was tied on a standard dry-fly hook and all there was to it was a sparse blue-dun hackle wrapped at the bend, a neat black thread body, and another sparse dun hackle at the hook eye.

"These may be Knotted Midges, but where I come from we just call it a Fore-and-Aft. It's been around forever," I said. It's not the sort of thing to say to a fly-tying machine who's your buddy, but he forgave me after a few weeks.

Actually, the fly wasn't a classic Fore-and-Aft because there was no tail, but I didn't tell my friend. Everything else was the same as on an old-fashioned Fore-and-Aft. In larger versions, it's one of those patterns that had its heyday but had been discarded by fly fishers for various reasons. Fly tiers probably discarded it because it was just too simple to tie.

DOWNSIZING OLD CLASSICS

In his classic book *Flies,* J. Edson Leonard referred to the Fore-and-Aft as a very high-riding imitation with one disadvantage. The pattern tends to roll on the water's surface, which puts the hook point in a variety of positions. That makes hooking trout problematic, especially with larger renditions of the pattern. Leonard's book was published in 1950, and he says that the Fore-and-Aft is "seldom seen today except when used on salmon and very rough and fast waters." That's pretty much the story today, with one exception, which is the so-called Knotted Midge.

The limited revival of the slightly modified Fore-and-Aft in microsizes makes sense. When tied on hooks size 20 and smaller, the disadvantage that Leonard talks about is pretty much a moot point. The fly is small enough so that even if the hook point is in an upward position, the odds are that you will hook up as often as you ever do when fishing midge patterns. More important is the action of the fly on the surface. It is a high rider that skates over the water at the least hint of a breeze. This skating, tumbling action can be just what the doctor ordered when you come across trout that are actually taking adult midges on the surface.

As much as I hate Latin, I have to say that the little Knotted Midge saved me once on a difficult hatch of Diamesinae. This particular midge subfamily is part of that huge family of midges known as the Chironomids. What caught my eye about these midges, which were hatching in the late winter, was that they were great skaters. The naturals were here and there all over the water's surface and the trout were chasing them. I fooled a few of those trout on a skated Knotted Midge imitation when no other pattern worked. And that's why I still keep a few Fore-and-Aft patterns—or if you're a romantic, Knotted Midges—in my fly box.

Instructions for tying the Knotted Midge are simple indeed. A standard dry-fly hook will suffice. If you have a preference for a turned-down eye or ring eye, go with it. Some of my friends think the ring eye allows the fly to roll around on the surface even better, but I don't think it's a factor. If you want to be picky, you could use a slightly smaller hackle on the rear of the fly, which will cock it up just slightly, but you don't have to. Some tiers mount the rear hackle with the dull side facing the rear, a trick that makes it a bit easier to wind the body material snugly up against it. However you wind it, good hackle is the key to the Knotted Midge because without a tail, the rear hackle is all that keeps the fly afloat. I make the thread body as slim as possible.

KNOTTED MIDGE

Hook: Standard dry fly, sizes 18 to 24.

Thread: Black 8/0 to 14/0.

Rear hackle: Dun.

Body: The tying thread.

Front hackle: Dun.

Note: Colors can be varied to match the midges on your favorite streams.

Roger Hill, a dedicated South Platte River small-fly fisherman, turned me on to a variation of the Fore-and-Aft that has worked well for him in Colorado. It's the venerable western fly known as the Renegade. Hill ties the Renegade, which is typically tied in larger hook sizes, on size 18 and smaller hooks. I first learned about the Renegade from Jack Dennis's *Western Trout Fly Tying Manual*, where he describes it as a "top producing rainbow trout fly." Of course, he described tying it on size 4, 6, and 8 long-shank hooks, but he did leave the door open for sizes as small as 18.

A Fore-and-Aft tied without a tail and in small sizes is sometimes called a Knotted Midge. It's a high floater that works well when trout are taking adult midges.

RENEGADE

Hook: Standard dry fly, sizes 18 to 22.
Thread: Black 8/0 to 14/0.
Tip (optional):   Gold Mylar tinsel.
Back hackle: Brown.
Body: Peacock herl.
Front hackle: White or cream.

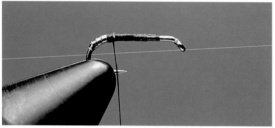

Step 1. Attach the thread and wind back to the bend. Tie in and wind the gold tinsel tag.

Step 2. Tie in two peacock herls where you want the rear hackle to end when you wind it. This somewhat unconventional approach (typically the hackle is tied on and wrapped, and then the peacock is tied in) is useful for small hook sizes where the hackle can be damaged if the peacock is tied in after it has been wrapped.

Step 3. Attach the rear hackle.

Step 4. Wind the hackle to where the peacock herl is tied in. Tie it off and clip the feather tip. Wind the peacock herl forward and tie it off.

Step 5. Clip the excess peacock herl, attach the front hackle, wind it forward, and tie it off.

The Renegade has a brown hackle aft and a white or cream hackle forward. The body is peacock herl, and the original pattern has a small gold tag. The most obvious advantage of the Renegade is that it's highly visible on the water. The action is much like that of a standard Fore-and-Aft, and I've found it effective with midging trout and as a miniature attractor pattern. The same tying rules that apply to the Fore-and-Aft apply to the miniature Renegade. Examine your supply of peacock herl closely when tying the Renegade to find herl with flue short enough to let you keep the body in proportion. If the flue is too long, it can actually fill the gap of a small hook when wrapped around the shank. An entire peacock tail feather will have herl with flue of various lengths and densities. I often find shorter flue lengths on stems closer to the butt of the feather.

I discovered another classic fly pattern that has been adapted to small sizes during the blue-

Step 6. Form a head and whip-finish the thread.

The flue on a piece of peacock herl varies in length. If the flue is too long, it can fill the gap of a small hook. A typical peacock tail feather has herl with a variety of flue lengths and densities. The very long flue on the herl to the left may not be suitable for tying small flies. Look for herl with a shorter flue (middle and right) closer to the butt of the tail feather.

winged olive hatch in the lower Cheeseman Canyon section of the South Platte River. There is a long flat there where the trout rise when the olives come off. They are some of the most difficult fish in the canyon. Every year for the past five or six years, I've seen an older man with white hair and a thin, white beard fishing the hatch on the flat. He always has his dog with him. The dog lies quietly on the shore while he casts, but if he gets a trout on, the dog stands up and watches. When the fish is released, the dog lies back down.

I eventually met this man a few years ago. He was catching trout right and left. As much as I tried, I couldn't even get a strike. I'd run through all my match-the-hatch standards such as size 22 CDC (cul-de-canard) loop-wing emergers, CDC dry flies, minute Quigleys, tiny quill-bodied parachutes, and the size 20 thorax flies that have always worked in the past. The trout wouldn't have anything to do with any of them.

Finally, I walked down to the man and asked what he was using. He stared at me for a few seconds. I had on my worn but still fancy Gore-Tex waders and a frayed fishing vest, and I was carrying a favorite split-cane fly rod. I looked like your standard, if somewhat rumpled, yuppie fly fisher. The old guy had rubber hip waders, blue jeans, a minimalist fishing vest, and a graphite fly rod.

We talked for a bit. He was retired and came to the canyon "a lot of days each week." I can vouch for how well he fished it.

The fly he handed me was an oddball version of the beloved Quill Gordon on a size 18 hook. The tail was blue-dun hackle barbs; the abdomen was the standard stripped and lacquered peacock quill. But the difference was up front. There was a peacock-herl thorax. He had wound a sparse, slightly oversize light-blue-dun hackle through the peacock and mounted sparse split wood-duck-flank wings in *front* of the hackle.

He would cast the fly down and across to the rising fish, with deadly results. It was larger than the naturals by a fair amount, but that didn't seem to matter. I tied on the fly he gave me and mimicked what he did. I missed the first strike because the fly wasn't easy to see on the water's surface, but I hooked up on the next. After that I put the fly away to use as a model at my tying bench.

When I was getting ready to walk up out of the canyon the old guy said, "Nice cane rod." I've met him on the river a number of times since, and all we talk about is fly fishing. I don't even know his name.

The little modified Quill Gordon has worked for me during a variety of small mayfly hatches on a number of rivers over the years. If tying the wings in front of the hackle disturbs your classic dry-fly design sensibilities, simply make a few wraps of hackle in front of the wings. I tie the wings up front because it reminds me of the gentleman who gave me the fly. It floats just fine.

ODDBALL QUILL GORDON

Hook:	Standard dry-fly hook, size 18 or 20.
Thread:	Black 10/0 Gudebrod.
Wing:	Lemon wood-duck flank or equivalent.
Tail:	Light blue dun.
Abdomen:	Stripped peacock quill, lacquered (optional).
Thorax:	Peacock herl.
Hackle:	Light blue dun.

Note: If you're tying a few of these flies, use a pencil eraser to "erase" the flue off the stem. It's quick and works well. Art Flick used to put a very small drop of head lacquer at the base of the V of the wood-duck wings after he divided them. He then smoothed it up through the wings. It "cements" the fibers together, keeping them out of the way when you're winding the hackle. Once the fly is complete, simply rub the lacquer out with your fingers or run a needle point up through the wings to separate the fibers. It works great and, in Art Flick's words, will help you tie "a wing you will be proud of."

Step 1. Tie in a clump of well-marked, lemon-colored wood-duck flank with one or two loose wraps, pull the fibers through the wraps to the proper length, and stand them up with wraps in front of and behind the wing.

Step 2. Apply a very small drop of head lacquer at the base of the wings. Smooth it through the wings.

Step 3. Slightly lacquering the wings cements the fibers together and will keep them out of the way when the hackle is wrapped.

Step 4. Tie in the tail.

Step 5. Tie in a stripped peacock herl and wrap it forward.

Step 6. Tie in the hackle and the peacock-herl thorax.

Step 7. Wind the peacock herl forward to the base of the wings and tie it off.

Step 8. Wind the hackle to the base of the wings, tie it off, and clip the feather tip. Advance the thread in front of the wing.

Step 9. Form a head and whip-finish the thread.

I think one of the secrets of the fly is the oversize hackle and the down-and-across presentation. The pattern skips and daps over the water's surface like a little Variant. And that attracts the trout's attention.

The Gold-Ribbed Hare's Ear, one of the all-time great general-purpose patterns, is another fly that made a successful transition to small sizes. F. M. Halford favored a rendition of it as a "floating fly" for dry-fly fishing, although by today's standards we would probably class it more as an emerger; it was fished on the surface or at least in the surface film. Ed Schroeder has come up with a modern equivalent in his Parachute Hare's Ear. The body of the fly is dubbed with spiky blended hare's ear, which is the secret of the fly's success whether you float it in the surface film on a parachute hackle or submerge it as a weighted Gold-Ribbed Hare's Ear nymph. The coarse dubbing traps tiny air bubbles that add flash to the pattern. Trout like that.

Over the years I've used a variety of Gold-Ribbed Hare's Ear nymph spin-offs in small sizes. The Flashback Hare's Ear uses a strand of pearlescent Mylar as a wing case or to cover the top of the abdomen and wing case. You can also slap a 2mm brass beadhead at the eye of the hook to add weight and flash.

My favorite small-fly rendition of the Gold-Ribbed Hare's Ear is tied very small on a size 22 or 24 Tiemco TMC 2488H hook. I use just a bit of gold-tipped, black hare's-mask guard hairs for the tail. The abdomen is light hare's ear. The rib is a single strand of pearlescent Krystal Flash. I use a barb or two of bronzy, black wild-turkey tail for the wing case, but any dark material will do. The thorax, also of light hare's ear, is picked out slightly. I also tie a dark version with dark hare's ear, but the light version is more effective.

The Flashback Hare's Ear is very effective when tied in small sizes. The pearlescent Mylar flashback can be used to cover just the wing case or the entire back, as on the fly pictured here.

TINY HARE'S EAR

Hook:	TMC 2488 or TMC 2488H, size 22 or 24.
Thread:	Black 10/0 Gudebrod.
Tail:	Black-tipped hare's-mask guard hairs.
Rib:	One strand of pearlescent Krystal Flash.
Abdomen:	Light hare's-ear dubbing.
Wing case:	Bronzy black turkey quill.
Thorax:	Light hare's-ear dubbing (picked out).
Note:	It won't hurt if your pattern is a little "messy." A Hare's Ear should look a little rough—it will catch more trout.

I don't know what this little Hare's Ear imitates. It could pass for a tiny caddisfly, a microscud, or even an emerging mayfly. It's the epitome of the general-purpose small fly. It has saved my bacon time and again on tailwaters and spring creeks throughout the Rocky Mountain region.

Jim Auman, a respected South Platte fly fisherman, helped me fine-tune another well-known larger fly pattern, the Muskrat Nymph, into a hot small-fly imitation. He says that dubbing technique is the key to tying small flies. Jim ties a very simple muskrat- or beaver-dubbed nymph that consists of a very thin abdomen with just the slightest "bump" of dubbing added for a thorax.

The Tiny Hare's Ear.

BEAVER OR MUSKRAT NYMPH

Hook: TMC 100 or similar dry-fly hook, size
           18 or smaller.
Thread: Black 8/0 to 14/0.
Abdomen: Beaver or muskrat dubbing.
Thorax: Beaver or muskrat dubbing.

"The trick is to just *dust* the tying thread with dubbing. Use as little as possible. It keeps the profile slender and adds translucence to the pattern," Auman says.

Auman picks the dubbing out a bit on each side of the thorax so that it trails back over the abdomen. Some tiers refer to this as an illusion of legs, but whatever you call it, it imparts just a little action to the fly—and that's good.

Most of these oldies are reminders of the not-so-long history of small flies. For all practical purposes, flies smaller than size 18 didn't come into widespread use until the late 1960s, when reliable small hooks became more readily available. Many of the first small-fly patterns were nothing more than downsized copies of well-know larger classic flies. I like carrying copies of some of these early small-fly patterns because they remind me of the relatively short history of small flies and how far pattern development has come in thirty years.

Besides, they work.

CLASSIC SMALL-FLY PATTERNS

Every small-fly aficionado has a few Griffith's Gnats in his box. The Griffith's Gnat is simple to tie and still as effective as ever. It's typically tied on a dry-fly hook from size 18 to 28. The peacock body is hackled palmer-style with a small grizzly feather.

You might wonder why I even mention what is probably the most frequently tied small fly in the world. I would agree, except that it's important to note one material change that can affect the efficiency of this fly.

The Beaver/Muskrat Nymph.

GRIFFITH'S GNAT

Hook: Standard dry-fly hook, sizes 18 to 26.
Thread: Black 10/0 Gudebrod.
Hackle: Grizzly.
Body: Peacock herl. After wrapping the body, palmer the hackle over it.

Ernest Schwiebert writes convincingly about the tiny Griffith's Gnat and about its creator, George Griffith, the founder of Trout Unlimited, in his books *Nymphs* and *Trout*. If you read carefully, you will note that Schwiebert believes the fly, which doesn't look like a midge at all, imitates a hatching midge that is "still tangled in its tiny pupal skin." He then says it fishes best when half awash in the film.

Here's my point. The quality of hackle, particularly small hackle, has improved so dramatically since Griffith came up with his Gnat that newer versions tied with genetic hackle may never get awash in the film, but rather float like corks on the stiff hackle tips. This doesn't mean the fly won't be effective in almost the same manner as the Fore-and-Aft—as an adult midge imitation, that is—but it could lose its appeal as a pupa imitation in the film.

For that reason, I tie some of my Griffith's Gnats with hackles from a precious, not-quite-so-stiff grizzly neck that I obtained back in the days before every fly shop carried genetic super hackle. It may or may not make a difference, but my "original" version Griffith's Gnats do sit down in the film a little better, and I think that's a plus. If you have any softer grizzly hackle in small sizes lying around, you might want to try it. Also, be sure to select peacock herl that has short fibers so that you can make a properly proportioned body.

You might also want to add some simple, palmered small-fly patterns in a variety of colors

This venerable pattern continues to take trout across North America. Tying it with a less-than-premium hackle will let it settle into the surface film.

The Griffith's Gnat style can be tied in many colors. A light version (pictured here), a dark version, and an olive-colored pattern should be in every midge fisherman's box.

to your box. I like a light tan body pattern palmered with a dirty white or light ginger hackle. An olive body with dun, ginger, or grizzly hackle can also be effective. Once again, a somewhat softer hackle might not hurt. If you use top-quality genetic hackle, you can make fewer wraps or wind a shorter hackle to help the fly float in the film rather than up on its toes.

No rundown of classic small-fly patterns would be complete without Ed Shenk's No-Name Midge. In Art Flick's *Master Fly-Tying Guide,* Ed Koch describes the No-Name as a

"little grizzly hackled gray-bodied size 20 fly." And it is that simple. It's basically a downsized dry-fly variant.

Shenk used muskrat to make the imitation's tapered body. The tail was a few grizzly hackle fibers and the hackle was grizzly. I'll admit to casting the No-Name Midge less frequently than I used to, but just last season it served me well during a hatch of minute blue-winged olives. It has also held its own on midge hatches over the years.

NO-NAME MIDGE

Hook: Standard dry-fly hook, sizes 18 to 26.

Thread: Black 8/0 to 14/0.

Tail: Grizzly hackle fibers.

Body: Muskrat fur.

Hackle: Grizzly.

Note: You can tie this fly with a thread body or with a trailing shuck in place of the tail. Don't hesitate to experiment with colors and materials.

The No-Name is also one of those patterns that just begs for modification. The idea of a trailing shuck of Z-Lon, Krystal Flash, muskrat, or any number of other materials is enticing. A slim thread body in black or olive can also be effective. I tie some No-Names with no tail at all. It's a basic pattern, but that doesn't diminish its effectiveness. As all small-fly aficionados know, catching trout on minute flies is easily as much a question of presentation as fly pattern.

This Ed Shenk pattern, essentially a traditional dry without wings, typifies a midge style that was popular years ago. It's still an excellent fly.

STRIPPED PEACOCK AND HERL

Hook: TMC 2487 or TMC 2488, size 18 or
             smaller.
Thread: Black 8/0 to 14/0.
Abdomen: Stripped peacock herl.
Thorax: Peacock herl.

A knowledge of materials preparation is the key to tying the familiar Stripped Peacock and Herl pattern. Jim Auman likes to tie this simple fly with the stripped peacock body and peacock-herl collar on a Tiemco TMC 2487 in smaller sizes. Most fly tiers know that a peacock herl can be easily stripped by simply running a pencil eraser over each side to remove the flue. What you may not know is that if you get an entire peacock tail feather you can find a variety of stem widths. If you want a thinner quill, look toward the eye of the feather.

The Stripped Peacock and Herl.

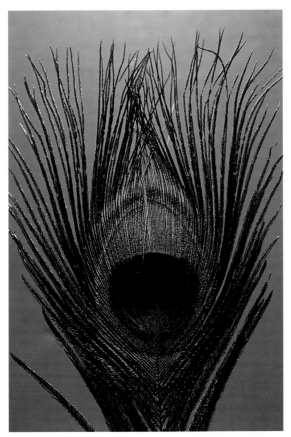

A complete peacock tail feather bears herls of various widths. The strands near the eye of the feather usually have narrower quills than the rest and are best for stripped-quill bodies on tiny flies.

NEWER IDEAS THAT WORK

The Buckskin, a well-known western tailwater pattern used to imitate microcaddis larvae or possibly small scuds, is a perfect example of how the preparation of a fly-tying material before it's mounted on the hook is sometimes more important than how many different materials you can stack onto a hook shank. At first glance, the fly looks deceptively simple to tie. It's nothing more than a few fibers of mottled cinnamon hen for a tail and a strip of buckskin wound around the shank of the hook for a body. You might think the Buckskin is easy to tie until you sit down at

the vise. That's when you realize that without proper preparation, the body of your small Buckskin will turn out way too bulky.

My friend Neil Luehring, who lives in Colorado Springs, is an accomplished small-fly angler and commercial fly tier. He's also considered the undisputed expert on how to tie the Buckskin.

"A buckskin hide has a smooth side and a rough, or suede, side," Neil says. He points out that the smooth side of the buckskin provides the strength in the material when it is stretched and wound around the hook. The suede side provides the unique segmented appearance of the fly. Luehring likes the suede to have a fine texture with a short nap. When looking at a piece of buckskin from the side, the suede should be about 30 percent of the width, with 70 percent of the width being smooth material.

Before you can tie the Buckskin pattern, the material must be cut into strips. Luehring suggests using a sharp razor and straightedge to cut the strips. It's best to cut the strips on a small piece of glass. "The glass is used as a cutting board because it allows the material to slide as it stretches during the cutting," Luehring says.

For smaller flies in sizes 16 to 20, Luehring cuts the strips to approximately a $1/16$ of an inch, but he cautions that the width may have to vary depending on the fly size and the characteristics of the particular piece of buckskin you are working with. Even for very small flies, the strips don't have to be extremely thin because they will slim down when stretched.

When it comes to the actual cutting, the straightedge is used to expose the desired width of buckskin, and the razor is then drawn in a smooth motion along the straightedge. Once the strips are cut, they should be run between your fingers to smooth them and stretch them. That makes each strip easier to control when wrapping it around the hook shank.

Luehring says that every piece of buckskin has a grain (like wood), and it's important to determine which direction of cut will provide the most strength in the buckskin strips. This is done by cutting a test strip or two from across the top of a square of buckskin and then from along one of the sides of the square. Test the strips by running them through your fingers and stretching them. You'll find that one of the strips will tend to stretch nicely, while the other will break or not stretch well. You want the strip that stretches. Once the grain is determined, all strips should be cut in that direction. Strips of about four inches are easy to work with and will usually make about four size 20 Buckskins.

Once the buckskin is cut and stretched, you are ready to tie the fly. For smaller patterns, Luehring uses dark brown 8/0 thread and a Tiemco TMC 3761 or an equivalent 1X-long nymph hook. The thread is tied in at the hook eye and wrapped back to the bend, where the hen fibers are tied in as a tail. The tail length should be about the width of the hook gap.

Next comes the final preparation of the buckskin for tying. First, hold the buckskin strip between your fingers with the suede side up.

With a sharp pair of scissors, cut the buckskin at about a 10-degree angle that comes to a point at the smooth side. Use the scissors to trim the fuzzy edge of the suede for about one inch. Trimming the suede down is how you reduce the bulk of the fly. This is especially crucial when tying on small hooks.

The very tip of the pointed end of the buckskin strip is then tied in at the tail and the thread brought forward about three-quarters of the way up the hook shank. The buckskin strip is wrapped around the shank with the *smooth* edge forward so that it lies against the shank. Luehring adjusts the body thickness by the degree of overlap on each wrap. When you reach the three-quarters point, tie off the buckskin. It's important to cut the buckskin as close to the hook shank as possible. This is best achieved by bringing the final wraps of thread over the shank at a slight angle and then closely trimming along that angle with your scissors. The thread is then wrapped over the cut end so that it forms a taper to the eye of the hook, where it is tied off.

BUCKSKIN

Hook:	TMC 3761 or equivalent 1X-long nymph hook, size 18 or smaller.
Thread:	Dark brown 8/0 to 14/0.
Tail:	Mottled cinnamon hen fibers.
Body:	Buckskin strip.

Step 1. Cut the deerskin with a single-edged razor. Work on a piece of glass, and use a metal straightedge to guide the blade. Each strip should be no more than $1/16$ of an inch wide.

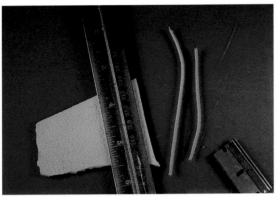

Step 2. Deerskin has a grain. After cutting your first strip, pull it between your fingers. It should feel stretchy. If the strip doesn't want to stretch or breaks easily, turn the piece of hide 90 degrees and cut another strip.

Step 3. Taper the end of each strip at a shallow angle. Trim about an inch of the fuzzy "suede" side of the strip with your scissors.

Step 4. Attach the tail.

Step 5. Attach the deerskin strip by the tip. Advance the thread about three-fourths of the way up the shank.

Step 6. Wrap the strip with the smooth edge forward. The shaggy edge faces rearward. The thickness of the body is determined by how much each wrap overlaps the preceding one.

Step 7. Tie down the strip at the front of the hook, cutting it at an angle and as close to the thread wraps as you can. Finish the head of the fly.

This may sound complicated for a fly using only two materials (hen fibers and buckskin), but it's a good example of how material selection and preparation can really make the difference in a small fly. With a little bit of practice, you will be tying effective Buckskins quickly and with ease.

THE ALL-AROUND *BAETIS*

Over the years, my friend A. K. Best and I have made it a point to meet on the South Platte River in the early autumn, when a difficult end-of-the-season hatch of very tiny mayflies occurs. It's every fly fisher's nightmare—which, of course, is precisely why it delights A. K., who is a dedicated match-the-hatch fly fisher. These mayflies hatch at high noon on bright sunny days. The trout rise freely to the emergers, duns, and, later in the day, the minute spent spinners. Fly fishers who fish this hatch wring their hands a lot and look up at the sky in hopes of divine intervention.

The main ingredient of the hatch is a dark blue quill (*Paraleptophlebia*). Although similar to a little blue-winged olive, the "paraleptos" don't quite fit the bill. The dun is brown, verging on a dark cinnamon, and is about a size 22. The spinner has a unique white abdomen with a tiny black segment at the tip of the tail. It's a striking mayfly with red eyes.

After getting skunked handily the first time we came across the hatch, both A. K. and I developed imitative patterns that have worked reasonably well when the trout are on top. It's still a difficult hatch, though, if only because the mayflies are coming off skinny water in the middle of bright autumn days.

One morning when I was waiting around for the hatch, I noticed that the trout were going nuts on nymphs. There were fish flashing and slashing everywhere under the riffles and in the shallow runs. I decided to fish nymphs and took several trout on a Pheasant Tail. A few days later I was fiddling around at the fly-tying desk and decided I'd try to make a closer imitation.

One of the tricks I use when working on a new small-fly pattern is to tie it on a somewhat larger hook so I can see how it's going to look. If I like it, I reduce it to the proper size. This particular imitation ended up on a size 18 hook. I'd looked at a few of the naturals on the river but hadn't saved any, so I wasn't all that clear on exactly what the colors were. I eventually decided to use brown hackle barbs for the tail and made a body of light muskrat. For flash, I tied a piece of

pearlescent Mylar over the entire back and ribbed it with fine gold wire. At the head I made a couple of wraps of a soft, blue feather from a California quail pelt I had lying around.

The resulting fly didn't really look like what it was supposed to. It was too gray, but it caught my eye anyhow. I liked the sort of wet fly/emerger look it had. I tied a few more. I never reduced the size of the new fly to that of the natural because it was past exact imitation. It was now in the realm of the general-purpose nymph with a very abstract origin in the "paralepto" hatch.

ALL-AROUND *BAETIS*

Hook:	Standard dry-fly hook, sizes 18 to 22.
Thread:	Black 10/0 Gudebrod.
Tail:	Brown hackle barbs.
Rib:	Fine gold wire.
Body:	Muskrat and narrow pearlescent Mylar.
Hackle:	Blue body feather from quail, or any similar soft blue feather.

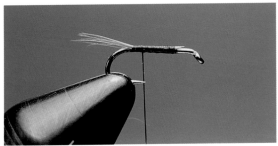

Step 1. Tie in the tail.

Step 2. Tie in the pearlescent Mylar and the wire, with which you'll form the rib.

Step 3. Dub the body.

Step 4. Pull the Mylar over the body and tie it down. Clip the excess Mylar. Wind the wire forward to form the rib. Tie off the wire and clip the excess.

Step 5. Mount the hackle.

Step 6. Make one or two wraps of hackle, tie off the feather, clip the excess, and form a neat thread head. Whip-finish, and clip the thread.

I took it to the river anyway and rigged it as the point fly on a two-fly dead-drift nymphing rig. The answer to how the fly would fare came within a few casts. The trout loved it. I couldn't believe it, because I'm not usually one of those fly tiers who comes up with patterns that actually produce. The icing on the cake was when a nearby fly fisher came up and asked what I was using. I gave him one of the flies and he started hooking up, too.

It turns out that the actual nymphs the trout were taking when I fished the fly that day were a medium tan color and about a size 22. My fly, when wet, was much darker and, of course, larger.

There are two ways to interpret why the fly was effective. The first is that there was a component in the dressing that triggered the trout. Even though the imitation was too large, the wrong color, and nothing like the natural, it may be that the flashy back alone was all the trout were really looking for—nothing else mattered. I've seen this happen before—a fly pattern doesn't *have* to resemble the natural much at all if it contains a trigger. The problem is that you can go nuts trying to figure out what it is about a bug or a hatch that triggers a trout. You have to believe that you can think like a trout. My standard rule for dealing with anglers who tell me they can think like a trout is to back away slowly from them without making any sudden moves or ever letting them out of my sight.

The second possibility for my nymph's effectiveness is that I had stumbled onto a general-purpose fly pattern. If I had, it would have been a bit like winning the lottery. All of a sudden, my fly could have ended up in the same category as the Pheasant Tail, Adams, Gold-Ribbed Hare's Ear, or Clouser Minnow. In fly tying, this doesn't happen much.

And it didn't happen with my fly, either. But the second best thing did. I made it a point to fish the pattern a little every time I was on the river, and I found that it was effective any time *Baetis* or similar small flies, like the *Paraleptophlebia,* were a factor. It had the same effect on rivers other than the South Platte, too.

CHAPTER SEVENTEEN

Guide's Choice

Like most fly shops, my neighborhood shop in Colorado Springs has one wall lined with fly bins. There is a small section right in the middle that has an unobtrusive sign that reads, "Guide Flies." These flies have either been invented by local guides or are recommended by them for our nearby waters. I was eyeballing the bin one day for the same reason that most of the fly fishers who come into the shop eyeball it. We are all always on the lookout for that extra edge and we assume the guides have it. Actually, it may even go farther than that. It could be that what we all are really looking for is the mythical "silver bullet."

The Guide Flies section tells a lot about our local fishing. I don't think I saw a fly larger than a size 18 in the bunch. This makes sense, because I live within an hour's drive of three separate tailwater sections of the South Platte River. If you extend that range to two hours, the number of tailwaters doubles. And if there is any single truth for Rocky Mountain tailwaters, it is that small-fly species are the bread-and-butter food for trout.

A closer examination of the Guide Flies revealed another interesting fact. The majority of the flies are imitations of midge larvae and midge pupae. That makes sense when you consider that

midge larvae can number in the tens of thousands per square yard of streambed in a rich tailwater.

The preponderance of these tiny midges means several things to fly fishers. Since midges are so small, trout need to eat a lot of them. Trout feed on them whenever they are available, which means most of the time because there are always some in the drift. And even if they aren't in the drift, the trout are used to seeing them there, so they are likely to take an imitation. In effect, the immature forms of midges, both larvae and pupae, form a year-round food source for tailwater and spring-creek trout. It only figures that fly-fishing guides are going to latch on to that potential.

The final thing I noticed in the Guide Flies bin was that a good number of the imitations were tied by Colorado Springs resident Stan Benton. Stan lived near the South Platte River for a number of years. He came about as close as you can to hard-wiring how to successfully dead-drift midge larva and pupa imitations to the trout. He also guided on the river for many of those years. It makes sense that he has come up with some unique midge patterns that have found their way to the Guide Flies bin.

Stan Benton's midge larva and midge pupa imitations (left to right): Macaw Midge, Stan's Blue Midge, Starling and Black, and Mr. Ed.

Stan's patterns go beyond basic midge larva and midge pupa imitations. As with all small flies, the keys to the effectiveness of Stan's flies are the materials and how those materials are used. Stan's patterns incorporate commonly used small-fly materials such as colored copper wire and synthetics, but he also utilizes less often seen materials such as blue-gold macaw feather, blue Krystal Flash, and horsetail hair—not your average small-fly stuff.

STAN'S BLUE MIDGE

Stan's Blue Midge is a standard design tied in a unique color. He uses a size 22 Tiemco TMC 2487 for the pattern. The abdomen is blue Krystal Flash. He recommends using two strands tied in at the rear of the hook and wrapped forward to the thorax area. This simply speeds up the tying process a bit. The thorax is dubbed with black/blue Arizona yarn, which is different from most dubbing materials because it has a flashy material in the yarn. Stan says that if you don't get any "flash" when pulling the yarn apart for dubbing material, it probably won't affect the productivity of the fly. Of course, a little extra flash never hurts.

STAN'S BLUE MIDGE

Hook: TMC 2487 or TMC 2488, size 22.
Thread: Black 8/0 to 14/0.
Abdomen: Two strands of blue Krystal Flash.
Thorax: Black/blue Arizona yarn.

Step 2. Wind the strands forward.

Step 1. Tie two strands of Krystal Flash to the hook shank.

Step 3. Dub the thorax. Form the head and whip-finish the thread.

What's interesting about the Blue Midge is how Stan came up with the pattern.

"I read an article where a study was done on dyed salmon eggs. The researchers found that trout eat blue-dyed salmon eggs over any background more often than they eat salmon eggs of any other color. That got me thinking about how I could incorporate that information into fly patterns where I fish," Benton says. The research reinforced what he'd found many years ago when he used to troll Lake Michigan for steelhead.

"We trolled for steelhead a lot and found that a blue-and-silver spoon was the best producer of any of the lures we had," Benton says. All he did was miniaturize the flashy blue effect to fit a size 22 hook.

"I won't tell you that the Blue Midge catches trout all the time, but there are days when it really is highly effective. It's especially good in the winter months. I couldn't tell you why," Stan says.

All I can say about the Blue Midge is that I was on the South Platte River late in the winter one year and nothing was working well. I switched to the Blue Midge and it saved the day. I caught trout on almost every decent dead-drift I made. It's one of the few times I can say that a fly imitation actually made the difference between catching trout or not. And that's difficult for me to say because I tend to believe that success lies in good presentations. On that day, the Blue Midge was as close to a silver bullet as I've ever seen. It's still among my most steady winter producers.

THE MACAW MIDGE

The color blue plays a role in Benton's Macaw Midge, too. "I was interested in tying salmon flies and got hold of this sack of blue-gold macaw tail feathers. As it turned out, only about two of them were salmon-fly quality. I decided to find something to do with the rest," Benton says.

He tied a barb from the tail feather of a macaw to a hook and found that when he wound it he got a yellow abdomen with a blue rib. "I was attracted to the blue color of the top side of the feather, but I ended up with this nice yellow body. I decided to stay with that," he says.

Benton ties the Macaw Midge on a size 18 Tiemco TMC 2487. The abdomen is a single barb from the macaw tail feather. It must be tied in with the blue edge facing toward the rear of the hook to get the blue rib. "It's just like winding a goose biot if you're trying to get a rib effect," Benton notes. The fly is finished with a short white Z-Lon wing and a black/blue Arizona yarn thorax.

MACAW MIDGE

Hook:	TMC 2487 or TMC 2488, size 18.
Thread:	Black 8/0 to 14/0.
Abdomen:	Single barb from a tail feather of a blue-gold macaw.

Wing:	White Z-Lon.
Thorax:	Black/blue Arizona yarn.

Step 1. Tie the macaw tail feather to the hook with the blue edge toward the rear.

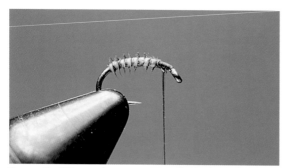

Step 2. Wrap the macaw tail feather forward, taking care to keep the blue edge toward the rear to produce a blue rib on a gold abdomen.

Step 3. Tie in the Z-Lon wing and trim to length.

"You shouldn't necessarily go out and buy the macaw, which can be a little expensive, but if you come across some or have excess from your salmon-fly tying, it makes a pretty good midge pattern. It's actually an emerger. I think it has the kind of flash that attracts the trout's attention," Benton says.

THE MR. ED

The impetus for the next Guide Fly, the Mr. Ed, was a stack of horsetail hair that Benton had lying around. "I was looking at the horsetail and noticed it had a nice sheen to it. It occurred to

Step 4. Dub the thorax. Form the head and whip-finish the thread.

me it might make a good abdomen for a midge pattern," he says.

Benton uses a size 18 Tiemco TMC 200R for the pattern. The abdomen is made by winding a single strand of black horsetail hair around the hook shank. Benton ties in a white goose biot by the tip on either side of the hook shank immediately after the abdomen. The tips are tied in pointing toward the hook eye. After he dubs the black beaver thorax, he pulls the biot over each side and ties it off at the head to create "breathers."

"The English have used breathers on their lake patterns for some time now, and there are a few small midge patterns tied in the States that use Z-Lon for a breather. The biot is very visible, and I've found that it's quite effective," Benton says.

Once the head is tied off, Benton coats the thorax and breathers with a thin layer of Softex for durability. "The horsetail seems to hold up fine, but the trout will tear up the biot if you don't use the Softex," he says.

MR. ED

Hook: TMC 200R, size 18.
Thread: Black 8/0 to 14/0.
Abdomen: Single strand of black horsetail hair.
Thorax: Black beaver.
Breathers: White goose biots.

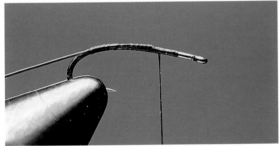

Step 1. Tie the horsetail hair to the hook.

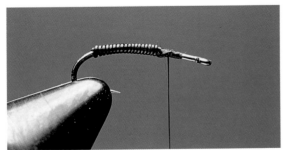

Step 2. Wind the horsetail forward. Tie it off and clip the excess.

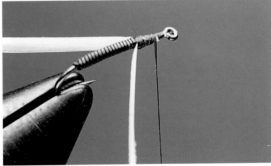

Step 3. Mount a white goose biot by the tip on each side of the hook shank.

Step 4. Dub the thorax.

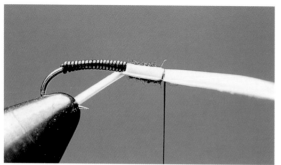

The Mr. Ed is one of several patterns I now carry that incorporate "breathers." I don't know if the trout actually perceive them as gills or if they simply add a little flash to the pattern. Whatever the reason, "breathers" on midge patterns do seem to improve performance, especially in heavily pounded tailwaters.

Step 5. Pull a goose-biot breather forward. Tie off the biot.

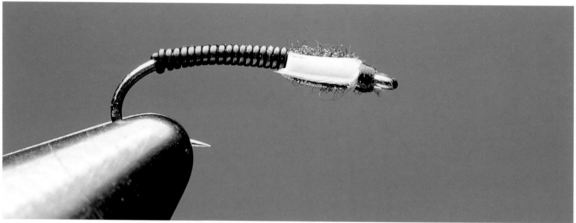

Step 6. Pull the other goose biot forward. Tie off the biot and clip the excess. Form a head and whip-finish the thread.

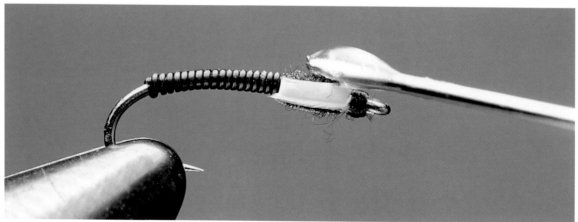

Step 7. Apply a thin coat of Softex to the thorax area.

THE STARLING AND BLACK

Stan Benton's final Guide Fly is the Starling and Black, which incorporates a wire body and bead-head to make an effective midge pupa imitation. He uses a size 18 Tiemco TMC 2487 hook to which he adds a 2mm black bead and black copper wire. The bead is threaded onto the hook first, then the wire is tied in behind the bead and wrapped over with thread to the rear of the hook. Stan leaves enough room at the bead so that when he whip-finishes over the wire, he can push the bead against it to leave room for a hackle. He then attaches thread in front of the bead, mounts a starling feather, makes two wraps, and ties the head off.

STARLING AND BLACK

Hook: TMC 2487 or TMC 2488, size 18.
Thread: Black 8/0 to 14/0.
Bead: Black 2mm.
Abdomen: Black copper wire.
Hackle: Starling.

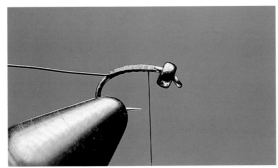

Step 1. Slip the 2mm bead onto the hook. Tie the black copper wire to the hook. Leave enough room to push the bead back over the wire and tie a hackle in front of it.

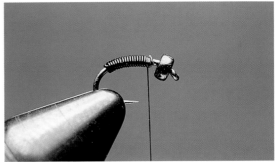

Step 2. Wind the wire forward to form a smooth body. Tie off the wire and clip the excess.

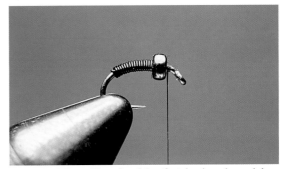

Step 3. Tie off and whip-finish the thread behind the bead. Slide the bead over the thread, then re-tie the thread to the hook shank in front of the bead.

Step 4. Mount the starling hackle in front of the bead.

"I take the small starling feather from the neck. It isn't especially easy to work with, and you may break a few off before you get the hang of it. I don't worry about wrapping it with the concave side to the front or rear because I like to smooth the hackle back a bit and tie it down in wet-fly fashion over the bead," he says.

When dead-drifting any midge larva or pupa pattern, Stan recommends that you suspend the imitation. "When the trout are actively feeding on larvae or pupae, you'll find them up off the bottom and at a specific zone in the water column. I like to suspend my imitation from a strike indicator so that it drifts right through that zone," he says.

This approach differs from the more common technique of attaching weight to the leader above the flies. The weight bounces along the streambed, and the fly then rises up into the water column. Whether it gets to the zone where the trout are is hit or miss. An angler must also detect the strike "through" the weight, which is bouncing along the streambed. Benton's technique eliminates the weight bouncing along the streambed because the fly is suspended directly in the zone. Strikes are easier to detect, and the fly spends more time in the zone where it can be seen by the trout. It makes sense.

Give these imitations a try or use them as inspirations to try new materials on your favorite midge larva and pupa patterns. Who knows—there may still be a silver bullet waiting to be discovered.

Step 5. Make two wraps of hackle. Form a head and whip-finish the thread.

CHAPTER EIGHTEEN

Poor Man's CDC

Jim Cannon called me a while back and said he had something he thought I should see. Jim's one of the most innovative tiers of small flies that I know, and when he talks, I listen. When I arrived at the shop where Jim works, the Blue Quill Angler in Evergreen, Colorado, he quietly escorted me into the fly-tying room, where he had set up a microscope.

"Take a look in here," he said.

I peered through the microscope and saw several fibers. Some were long and relatively straight, but others started fairly straight, then corkscrewed into tight kinks and finally ended in long, flat, curved stems.

"That's interesting," I said. "What is it?"

"It's hair from the foot of a snowshoe hare," Jim replied. "Or you could just call it poor man's CDC."

Jim described how he learned about snowshoe-hare fur by tying Francis Betters's highly regarded pattern called the Usual. Betters is best known for originating the Haystack, a no-hackle, deer-hair-wing imitation used as a model for the Compara-dun. Betters was experimenting with other types of hair for the Haystack when he came across a snowshoe hare's foot on his tying bench. He soon discovered that the hair on the bottom of the foot has unique properties and could serve as an alternative to deer hair in the Haystack. Further experiments led to the Usual. The story goes that Betters never named the fly, but that Beaverkill fly fisher Bill Phillips coined the name "Usual" for the fly.

OLD MATERIAL, NEW TREATMENT

The snowshoe hare, also known as the varying hare because its fur turns white in the winter, spends a lot of time on the snow. Not surprisingly, the bottoms of its feet are insulated from freezing. Cannon figures that's where the kinked hair comes in.

"You find more of that spongy, kinky hair toward the heel of the foot, where the hare's weight compresses the normal hair. The compression should cause it to lose its ability to insulate, but the kinky hair traps air for insulation and is wiry enough to keep the hare's weight from fully compressing it," he says.

Cannon noticed that the ability of this kinky hair to trap air is very reminiscent of a cul-de-canard feather. Some tiers believe that natural oils in the hair are the real secret behind its ability to

Snowshoe-hare flies float and hold up very well. If you prepare the material properly, they're easy to tie, too.

float. I view this claim with skepticism. I think both CDC and snowshoe-hare hair float well because the structure of the feather barbs or hair naturally traps air. It could be that natural oils enhance flotation, but even that is debatable.

The quality of the hair is not uniform along the bottom of the foot. Hair near the toe is usually longer, coarser, and contains fewer kinky hairs, but the middle section of the foot contains a mix of both straight and kinky hair. A typical foot varies in color from a light tan at the heel to a yellowish tan at the toe. The best hair on the foot exhibits a sheen or translucence and is most often found at the heel.

Cannon's initial experiments with the hair involved tying standard patterns of the Usual. These

recipes require the tier to cut the hair from the foot as needed for individual flies. Some patterns have wings made from the longer guard hairs cut from the toe and dubbed bodies made from the kinkier underfur. Another technique requires cutting the hair from the foot with curved-blade scissors (convex side facing down) and separating the material into three bunches: the longer guard hairs are set aside for making wings, a bunch of fine guard hairs and soft underfur is used for making tails, and a third bunch consisting almost solely of soft underfur is set aside for body dubbing. Most tiers get five to seven dozen Usuals from one snowshoe-hare foot.

Cannon noted that the process of cutting and separating the hair into bunches is tedious and

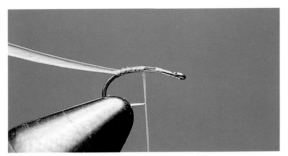

Step 1. Tie on the tip of a goose biot.

Step 2. Wind the biot to form a smooth abdomen.

Step 3. Tie an aligned bunch of snowshoe-hare dubbing parallel to the top of the hook shank.

Step 4. Dub a thorax of beaver underfur. Note that the thorax elevates the wing. Tie off at the head and whip-finish the thread.

Step 5. Trim the hair parallel with the hook shank to form a suspender-style wing, leaving some long hair in front.

Step 6. Finish trimming the hair.

Step 7. On this variation of the Snowshoe-Hare Emerger, a trailing shuck of cul-de-canard was tied in before the goose-biot abdomen was formed.

Cannon's Bunny Dun is commercially available in *Baetis,* pale morning dun, and Trico dun imitations. These flies are different from his other snowshoe-hare patterns. Instead of lying parallel to the hook shanks, the wings are tied perpendicular to the shanks with figure-eight wraps of thread around the base of the material. The raised wings are then trimmed to length.

BUNNY DUN

Hook:	TMC 101, sizes 18 to 26.
Thread:	8/0 to 14/0 in a color to match the natural insect.
Tail:	Betts Tailing Fibers or Microfibetts.
Abdomen:	Goose biot in a color to match the natural insect.
Thorax:	Beaver underfur in a color to match the natural insect.
Wing:	Snowshoe-hare dubbing in a color to match the natural insect.

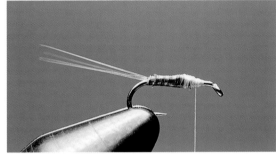

Step 2. Tie on the tip of a goose biot. Wind the biot to form a smooth abdomen.

Step 1. Tie in a divided tail. Use two fibers on each side of the hook for sizes 18 to 22. Use one fiber on each side for hook sizes 24 and 26.

Step 3. Use crisscross wraps to tie a bunch of snowshoe-hare dubbing perpendicular to the top of the hook shank. If you want the fly to imitate a spent spinner, complete the head and clip the thread. If you want the fly to imitate a dun, proceed as follows.

Step 4. Raise the wings and make several wraps around the base of the wings.

Step 6. Trim the wings to the proper length.

Step 5. Dub the thorax. Tie off the thread and whip-finish.

Step 7. The completed fly.

All of these patterns are indestructible, and they dry with just a few false casts. Cannon says that you can add even more "float" to the flies by crushing some desiccant crystals into a fine powder and rubbing the powder into the dubbing.

Cannon's tying techniques have changed the way I think about the snowshoe-hare and small flies. I used to consider snowshoe-hare fur a marginal material for tying on hooks smaller than size 20, but now I easily tie down to size 24. And what's more, the flies really work. Much like those with CDC, small-fly patterns tied with the snowshoe-hare dubbing are highly visible on the water's surface, which is a desirable characteristic in small flies. The patterns are also durable and easy to dry (unlike CDC patterns).

Simply put, Jim Cannon's snowshoe-hare dubbing really is poor man's CDC. That's something I can live—and fish—with.

CHAPTER NINETEEN

32s!

When I started fooling around with small flies thirty years ago, the push was always toward smaller and smaller patterns. It was an elemental quest. In our own way, as dedicated small-fly junkies, we were trying to split the fly-tying atom. I still have my first box of size 28 hooks. At the time, the straight-eye, round-bend, 1X-fine Mustad-Viking 94859 was about the smallest hook we could get, although there were rumors of sizes 30 and 32.

The reason I still have that first box of size 28 hooks is a bit complicated. Although we could tie size 28 flies back then, it was very difficult for tiers to find suitable hackle and other materials for such small patterns. We sometimes faked it by trimming size 22 or 24 materials to fit a size 28 hook. Considering the difficulties, it is surprising that we came up with patterns that caught any fish at all. Or I should say *hooked* any fish, because the real difficulty with the size 28s was that we would get strikes but were seldom able to get solid hookups. Most of the time we broke the trout off before we could bring it to net. Most of us eventually compromised by using size 22 and 24 hooks. We got fewer strikes, but we landed the trout more often.

None of this means that we didn't aspire to catching trout on smaller flies. Pennsylvanian Vince Marinaro set the standard in 1950 when he published *A Modern Dry-Fly Code* and again in 1976 when he published *In the Ring of the Rise*. Marinaro admitted in the introduction to the 1970 edition of *A Modern Dry-Fly Code* that when the book first came out he really didn't have fine enough gut to properly fish size 22 and smaller hooks, but that changed with the availability of small hooks and nylon tippet material as fine as 8X.

"But in those early days I was a prophet without honor, for I was severely challenged for even suggesting, as I did in chapter 3 , that size 14 was the largest that need be used for any dry-fly imitation," Marinaro said.

Marinaro would be impressed by what has transpired since the publication of *In the Ring of the Rise* in 1976. Low-bulk synthetics, very fine tying threads, cul-de-canard, genetic hackle, high-quality small hooks, and higher pound-test monofilament for lightweight tippets have made tying and fishing size 28 imitations practical. But the size 30—and smaller—hook-size barrier remained.

I tried to ignore the size 32 Tiemco TMC 518 hooks with the straight eye, 3X-fine wire, short shank, and snappy microbarb when they first appeared at my local fly shop. I did a pretty good job for a while, too, though I did sneak back to the hook display just to look at them once in a while.

How small is a size 32 hook? Pictured here are four size 32s dancing on the top of two pin heads. On the left, dry flies; on the right, subsurface 32s.

The final blow was the publication of Don Holbrook and Ed Koch's book *Midge Magic* in 2001. Holbrook routinely ties highly imitative flies down to size 26 and included a short chapter on flies tied on the TMC 518 size 32 hooks. So, yes, I bought a pack of the size 32s. And, yes, they will test your small-fly tying and fishing skills. Here's a primer on what I've learned about tying down to size 32.

TINY TOOLS AND MATERIALS

I use few specialized tools when I tie small flies but make some exceptions when working on size 32s. You'll need midge jaws in your fly-tying vise and probably some sort of magnification. I actually tie the flies without magnification, but I check my work with a 10X hand lens.

You'll also need the best scissors you can find. I cherish a pair of very sharp scissors that a surgeon gave me a number of years ago. In some cases, a sharp hobby knife or razor blade will cut materials closer than even the sharpest scissors.

Keeping bulk to a minimum is crucial when tying size 32 flies. Use Gudebrod 10/0 or Wapsi 70-denier tying thread. If I can get a good color match, I use the threads to form the fly body. Both brands of thread have floss-like characteristics that allow them to lie flat when wrapped. If a good thread-color match is not available, I dub the body with Umpqua Superfine Dry Fly dubbing or an equivalent. Dub the material as tightly as possible without waxing the thread. Wax just gunks things up. A tightly dubbed body creates a hint of segmentation.

Always avoid the hook point when wrapping dubbing or thread around the shank. The hook point will cut or fray the thread, and any fraying on a size 32 fly will stick out like a sore thumb. If the thread does fray, it's easier starting over than trying to recover.

HACKLED TINY MIDGE ADULT

Hook: TMC 518, size 32.
Thread: Black Gudebrod 10/0 or Wapsi 70-denier.
Body: Umpqua Superfine Dry Fly dubbing in a color to match the natural.
Hackle: Grizzly or barred-ginger hackle.

I usually make size 32 dry-fly wings out of cul-de-canard (CDC) feathers. CDC keeps the fly afloat and makes it more visible on the water's surface. Hackle will also keep the fly floating. I've found usable size 30 and 32 feathers on Whiting Farm's capes. Although it's possible to use genetic hackle to tie a size 32 No-Name Midge very similar to Ed Shenk's original pattern, I prefer the way a CDC wing allows the body of the fly to rest in the surface film. I use tan CDC for making wings because it's easy to see on the water and many midges in my area have tan wings when they hatch. White is my second favorite color for wings. I tie the wings in two different configurations: upright and down-wing. I use black thread to tie on the wing because it more closely imitates the thorax area of a newly hatched natural, and I tie the body out of thread or dubbing that matches the color of the insect. I initially thought that these tiny flies would need tails. My tests, however, proved they float fine without tails, and that the bodies hang nicely in the surface film.

It is possible to find genetic hackle as small as size 32, as demonstrated by the hackle on this size 32 dry fly.

TINY MIDGE ADULT WITH UPRIGHT WING

Hook: TMC 518, size 32.

Thread: Black Gudebrod 10/0 or Wapsi 70-denier.

Body: Chartreuse Gudebrod 10/0 thread, or Umpqua Superfine Dry Fly dubbing to match the natural.

Wing: Tan CDC.

Note: The Tiny Midge Adult may be tied with either an upright or a down wing. Use black thread to tie on the wing and form the thorax of the fly.

Step 2. Secure the wing with two or three tight wraps of thread, pull the wing tips up, and hold them in position by making as few wraps of thread as possible at the base of the fibers in front of the wing. Clip the CDC butts.

Step 1. Start the thread about one-third hook-shank length behind the eye. Select a CDC feather for the wing. Stroke the fibers toward the tip of the feather. The fiber tips should be about even. I prefer my wing a bit on the full side, so I don't use CDC feathers on which the individual fibers are too sparse. Cut away the bottom portion of the feather, and tie on the remaining fibers with the tips pointing out over the hook eye. The wing should be one and a half to two times the length of the hook shank. If the length isn't exactly right, pull the CDC fibers back under the thread until it is the proper length.

Step 3. Wrap the tying thread behind the wing and neatly wrap over the butt ends of the CDC fibers and whip-finish by hand behind the wing. Whip-finishing *behind* the wing ensures that the hook eye doesn't get closed with thread.

Step 4. Once the wing is posted upright and whip-finished, switch to another bobbin of the proper color thread to wrap the body. Wrap to the end of the hook and back again to the base of the wings. Whip-finish behind the wing and clip the thread to complete the fly.

The down-wing version of the fly begins at the back of the hook. Use dubbing or plain thread to tie a body covering two-thirds of the hook shank.

TINY ADULT DOWN-WING MIDGE

Step 1. Tie in the thread and make an abdomen by wrapping down the hook shank to the bend and then back up the shank. Whip-finish the body and switch to black thread to tie on the wing. Prepare the CDC in the same way you did for the upright-wing version.

Step 2. Tie in the wing with the tips rearward. The wing should be one and a half to two times the length of the hook shank. Leave enough room on the hook shank so you can pull up the butt ends of the CDC fibers and make several wraps under them.

Step 3. Raise the butt ends of the CDC fibers and make several wraps under them. This will lift the butt ends away from the hook shank and make them easier to trim with scissors or a razor blade.

Step 4. There will probably be a remaining bit of fuzz that looks similar to the head on an Elk Hair Caddis. Don't try covering the butt ends and risk closing up the hook eye with excess thread; just whip-finish *behind* them to complete the fly.

SIZE 32 SUBSURFACE FLIES

THREAD MIDGE

Hook:	TMC 518, size 32.
Thread:	Black Gudebrod 10/0 or Wapsi 70-denier.
Body:	Gudebrod 10/0 thread, olive or a color to match the natural.
Rib:	Black Gudebrod 10/0 thread, tightly twisted.
Note:	Build up the head with thread to imitate a pupa, or reduce the amount of thread to imitate larva.

You can make simple subsurface size 32s by matching the color of the natural insect with thread or dubbing, and making a rib with one or two turns of thread. (You might have to tightly twist the ribbing thread to prevent it from splaying and covering the body.) Add a wing case by either wrapping black thread or dubbing in the thorax area—but remember that on a size 32 fly, you can cover up the body if the wing case is too big. Try using imitations tied with and without wing cases. The trout often don't seem to care whether or not a fly this small has one.

The Thread Midge, size 32.

MIDGE PUPA

Hook:	TMC 518, size 32.
Thread:	Black Gudebrod 10/0 or Wapsi 70-denier.
Body:	Umpqua Superfine Dry Fly dubbing in a color to match the natural.
Wing case/thorax:	Black Umpqua Superfine Dry Fly dubbing.

I tie size 32s mostly because I'm a sucker for small flies, but I can report I have caught trout on both the dry-fly and subsurface size 32 versions. I can also report that I missed a number of hookups for the same reason I missed hookups on the old size 28s. But the new Tiemco TMC 518 hook is strong and well-designed. The gap is wide enough so that you can hook fish, and the eye will actually accept tippet material as large as 4X, though you'll want to use something considerably lighter. I'm beginning to think that these very, very small flies might actually work this time around.

The Midge Pupa, size 32.